BRIGHT
NEW IDEAS

Grammar and Punctuation Lifesavers

AGES 5-11

Sylvia Clements

Author
Sylvia Clements

Editor
Christine Harvey

Assistant Editor
Aileen Lalor

Project Editor
Wendy Tse

Series designer
Joy Monkhouse

Designer
Erik Ivens

Illustrations
Garry Davies

Cover photographs
© Getty Images

Published by Scholastic Ltd,
Villiers House,
Clarendon Avenue,
Leamington Spa,
Warwickshire
CV32 5PR

Printed by Bell & Bain Ltd, Glasgow

2 3 4 5 6 7 8 9 0   5 6 7 8 9 0 1 2 3

Visit our website at www.scholastic.co.uk

British Library Cataloguing-in-Publication Data
A catalogue record for this book is available from
the British Library.

ISBN 0-439-97135-7

Contents

Introduction   5

Chapter 1 – Parts of speech   7

My aunt's cat   7
Mixed bag!   8
Use your senses   9
All together now...   10
Capital cubes   11
Who am I?   12
The plurals game   13
The 'tell us' trees   14
How did they do it?   15
Up and over   16
Journey time   17
I've started, so you finish!   18
Points of view   19
Identikit   20
Are you sitting comfortably?   21
What can you do?   22
Up, up and away!   23
Sunshine and showers   24
Person to person   25
Lost property   26

Chapter 2 – Sentence construction   36

Cloud burst sentences   36
Spot the stop!   37
The subject sack   38
Double trouble   39
Complex definitions   40
Complex creations   41
Scene setting   42
Order, order!   43
If...   44
It happened like this...   45

Chapter 3 – Punctuation   53

Capital caterpillar   53
This is me!   54
Alphabet sentences   55
A capital collection   56
Next stop please!   57

Full stop flower power	58
I wonder and I wonder…	59
What a picture!	60
Who's asking?	61
Wow!	62
I say…	63
Character quotes	64
Quote me	65
Dialogue hunt	66
When I went on holiday…	67
Famous inserts	68
Colon completion	69
A tasty treat	70

Chapter 4 – Grammatical awareness and presentation

Chapter 4 – Grammatical awareness and presentation	**80**
Word detectives	80
Be positive!	81
That book were good!	82
Do you agree?	83
It's official!	84
Where's the emphasis?	85
As the saying goes	86
Let's get organised! (1)	87
Let's get organised! (2)	88
English through the ages	89

Introduction

Welcome to *Grammar and Punctuation Lifesavers*! This book contains a bank of lively activities for children in both Key Stages 1 and 2, which provide a stimulating approach to grammar and punctuation teaching and learning.

The book is divided into four chapters: Parts of speech, Sentence construction, Punctuation, and Grammatical awareness and presentation. All the features of grammar and punctuation, which are covered by the National Literacy Strategy (NLS), have been grouped and put into the appropriate chapter. A representative spread of objectives for each year group is covered by activities in this book.

Each activity is broken down into the areas outlined below.

Age range
Each activity specifies an age range. This may be a single year group, or a wider age range if the objective is revisited by another sentence level objective for revision purposes in a later year group. Most of the activities are suitable for mixed year group teaching.

Learning objectives
The activity objectives are based on the sentence level objectives detailed in the NLS. The table on page 6 details the NLS objectives covered in this book.

Curriculum links
Each activity specifies which NLS objective it covers and if there are any other links to different areas of the National Curriculum.

What you need
The materials needed for each activity are detailed under this heading.

What to do
Information for conducting each activity is presented in short bullet points. The details of each grammatical point are included to avoid the need to make reference elsewhere.

Differentiation
Suggestions for extending or adapting the activities for more able children and for providing support or adapting the activities for less able children are given.

Photocopiable pages
Many of the activities are supported by photocopiable pages. Suggestions for how to use each of these are given in each individual activity.

NLS sentence level objectives covered

Book chapter	Grammar/punctuation feature	Year R	Year 1 (5–6) Term 1	2	3	Year 2 (6–7) Term 1	2	3	Year 3 (7–8) Term 1	2	3	Year 4 (8–9) Term 1	2	3	Year 5 (9–10) Term 1	2	3	Year 6 (10–11) Term 1	2	3
Parts of speech	Adjectives (pages 7–9)									S2/3			S1							
	Nouns (pages 9, 10, 13, 26)									S4/5										
	Adverbs (pages 14–15)											S4								
	Prepositions (pages 16–17)															S3				
	Conjunctions (page 18)										S5									
	Connectives (page 19)													S4			S7	S4		
	Pronouns – capital letters for I and for names (pages 11, 12, 20)	S4	S5/9	S7		S5					S2									
	Verbs (pages 22–25)						S5		S3/4			S2/3	S2		S8					
	1st/2nd/3rd person (pages 21,25)														S8					
Sentence construction	Sentence construction – capital letters, full stops (pages 36–38, 43)		S5/6/7/8	S4/6	S6		S9		S10/11				S3							
	Clauses (pages 40, 42)																S6		S3	
	Conditionals (page 44)																		S5	
	Complex sentences (pages 41, 42)																	S5		S4
	Sentence contractions (page 39)															S7				
	Time phrases (page 45)										S6									
Punctuation	Capital letters (pages 53–56)	S4	S5/8/9	S4/7	S5	S5				S8										
	Full stops (pages 57, 58)		S5/8	S4/5																
	Question marks (pages 59–61)				S7			S6/7	S6											
	Speech marks (pages 63–66)						S6		S7		S4				S7					
	Commas (pages 67–68)					S3	S8	S4				S5			S6					
	Colons (page 69)													S2	S6					
	Semi-colons (page 70)													S2			S6			
	Exclamation mark (page 62)					S3			S6											
Grammatical awareness and presentation	Formal language (page 84)																		S2	
	Language investigations (page 86)																			S2
	Standard verb forms (page 83)										S3									
	Standard English (pages 81, 82)						S4	S3							S2	S2	S1			
	Active/passive voice (page 85)																S2			
	New vocabulary prediction (page 80)								S1/2/3	S1	S1									
	Captions, bold print (page 88)						S7		S9											
	Italics (page 88)							S7	S9											
	Arrows, lines, boxes, keys (page 87)					S6														

BRIGHT IDEAS

CHAPTER 1

Parts of speech

AGE RANGE 7–8

LEARNING OBJECTIVE
To understand the function of adjectives within sentences through collecting and classifying them; using dictionary skills.

CURRICULUM LINKS
National Literacy Strategy Year 3 Term 2

My aunt's cat

What you need
Soft toy cats or pictures of cats; a board and writing materials; dictionaries (enough for one between two); photocopiable page 27; writing and drawing materials; empty project book.

What to do
● A few days before the lesson, tell the children you want them to bring in a picture of a cat. Explain that this could be from a magazine, a photograph or a cartoon. If they have a soft toy cat, they could bring that in. Alternatively, have an art lesson where the children draw cartoon cats with different personalities and use these drawings.

● At the beginning of the lesson, select one of the cats and ask the class to describe it to you. Write on the board the children's descriptions, and explain that these words are adjectives – a word that describes a noun (the cat). Ask them to think of adjectives to describe the cat that they brought in. Keep collecting examples until everyone fully understands the concept of an adjective. Highlight the use of *an* for adjectives that begin with a vowel.

● Explain the game 'My aunt's cat' to the children. Tell them it is a game where an adjective for each letter of the alphabet is found to describe a cat.

● Put the children in pairs and give each pair a dictionary, a copy of photocopiable page 27 and writing materials.

● Explain to the children how to locate different parts of speech in a dictionary. Let them practice locating adjectives until they understand how to identify them.

● Read through the photocopiable sheet with the children and ensure they understand that they should work in their pairs to find adjectives for each letter of the alphabet to describe 'My aunt's cat'. They will undoubtedly find several for each letter, but encourage them to select their favourite before adding it to the sheet. This may be continued in a second session or the children can complete it for homework.

● When the children have finished, ask them to share their findings.

Differentiation
More able children should be encouraged to qualify their choice of adjectives and extend their sentence. Less able children could be given a limited number of letters to find adjectives for, using dictionaries suitable for their level of ability.

AGE RANGE 7–8

LEARNING OBJECTIVE
To construct adjectival phrases, and investigate comparative and superlative adjectives.

CURRICULUM LINKS
NLS: Year 3, Term 2; Year 4, Term 2

Mixed bag!

What you need
A blue bag labelled *Nouns*; a red bag labelled *Adjectives*; a word card with *flower* on; a board and writing materials; photocopiable page 28, the words copied onto card and cut out.

What to do
● Show the class the two bags and explain that they contain word cards. Explain that the blue bag contains the names of things and that these words are called nouns. Ask each child to pick a card from the bag, read it out, then put it to one side.

● Explain that the red bag contains describing words – words that can tell us what things are like. Explain that these are adjectives. Show them your own noun card – *flower*. Ask them to picture a flower in their heads. Explain that they will all be 'seeing' a different flower because you have not used adjectives to describe the flower yet.

● Ask a child to come up and draw the flower that you describe to them on the board. For example, *It has a <u>small</u>, <u>round</u>, <u>yellow</u> centre and <u>five</u> petals*. List the adjectives used on the board.

● Tell the children they are going to play a matching game. Ask a child to pick an adjective from the red bag and to read it out. Ask if anyone thinks that the adjective could be used to describe their noun, and if so, ask them to put the noun and adjective together in a sentence. Encourage the children to be as imaginative as possible. For example, *Lucy puffed as she climbed to the top of the <u>tall building</u>* is better than *It was a very <u>tall building</u>*. When a child has formed an imaginative sentence using their noun and the adjective, give them the adjective card.

● Repeat this, writing the sentences on the board each time. Help the children to develop their sentences, taking suggestions from the class.

● When everyone has matched their noun with an adjective this can be extended to develop the concept of comparative and superlative adjectives.

● Explain that comparative adjectives compare two examples, such as *The building Lucy climbed was <u>taller</u> than the Eiffel Tower*. Then explain that superlative adjectives describe the limit of something, such as *The Empire State Building was the <u>tallest</u> building Lucy had ever seen*. Invite the class to create sentences with comparative and superlative adjectives from their noun/adjective combination.

Differentiation
Appropriately directed verbal support and encouragement is required for this activity.

AGE RANGE 7–8

LEARNING OBJECTIVE
To understand the terms adjective and noun, and to know that an adjective qualifies a noun.

CURRICULUM LINKS
NLS: Year 3, Term 2

Use your senses

What you need

A large decorated cardboard box; a piece of material; a selection of different objects that will encourage the use of a wide range of adjectives to describe them, such as a teddy, a cabbage, a hairbrush, a sponge; bright cards with adjectives that relate to the objects; a table for a display; a board and writing materials.

What to do

● Before the lesson, prepare a small interactive display. Hang the cards with adjectives from the ceiling at different heights, so that the children can see them. These can support the children during the activity. Write 'Use your senses' on the board and stick a selection of adjectives around the board. Make a touchy feely box. Hang the piece of material over the open end of the box, to prevent the contents from being seen. Have your selection of objects close by.

● Begin the lesson by introducing the display to the children. Explain that you are going to put something in the touchy feely box and that you will ask a volunteer to use their sense of touch to work out what it is. Explain that we call the object in the box a noun. Explain that as the child feels the object, they should describe it before guessing what it is. The words they use to describe the object will be adjectives. Read out some of the adjectives in the display as examples.

● Put an object in the box without the children seeing. Choose a child to have a go and keep reminding them to describe the object before guessing what it is. List the adjectives they use on the board. When they have correctly guessed the object, reiterate that the object is the noun and the words used to describe it are adjectives. Place a different object in the box and pick somebody else to have a go.

● The display can be used when the children have completed a piece of work. Place new objects in the touchy feely box and let the children work in pairs to describe the objects and collect new adjectives.

Differentiation

Less able children could be given a range of adjectives on cards to choose from when using the touchy feely box. More able children could be encouraged to use a thesaurus to find a wider range of adjectives.

AGE RANGE 7–8

LEARNING OBJECTIVE
To understand the term *collective noun*, collect examples and invent their own; to recognise the use of singular and plural forms and identify those which cannot be pluralised.

CURRICULUM LINKS
NLS: Year 3, Term 2

All together now...

What you need
Photocopiable page 29 photocopied onto card four times and cut up; 15 large circles of card with Blu-Tack on the back; a whiteboard and marker pens; hall space.

What to do
● Recap the definition of a noun with the class and quickly collect some examples. Explain that nouns can be singular (just one) or plural (more than one) and that sometimes there is a special name for groups of things – *collective noun*.
● Take the class into the hall and sit them in a circle with the circles of card spread out in the centre. Explain that they are going to find out the names for different groups of things – the collective nouns.
● Hand out all the pictures from the photocopiable sheet (each child should have about four different pictures).
● Begin by asking one child to select a circle of card and pin it to the whiteboard. Then ask them to stick one of their pictures to it. Explain that at the moment there is just one, for example, bee on the card and that the singular is *One bee*. Write this on the card.
● Ask if anyone else has a bee and invite a child to come up and stick their picture onto the card. Explain that now there are two bees, and that this is the plural. Write *Two bees* on the card.
● Next ask anyone else with a picture of a bee to come and stick it on the card. Now that there are lots of bees ascertain that the collective noun for many bees is a swarm. Write the phrase *A swarm of bees* on the bottom of the card.
● Place the completed card back in the middle of the circle.
● Ask another child to take a piece of card to the white board and stick one of their pictures onto it. Repeat the process, confirming the singular, plural and collective forms of the noun and adding them onto the card.
● Highlight the examples which cannot be pluralised, for example, sheep and fish.

Differentiation
Put the children in mixed ability pairs and write a selection of plural nouns on the board for the children to make up their own collective nouns for. For example, A _____ of clocks.

AGE RANGE 5–7

LEARNING OBJECTIVE
To recognise and use capital letters for names, places, months and dates.

CURRICULUM LINKS
NLS: Year R; Year 1, Terms 1, 2 and 3; Year 2, Term 1

Capital cubes

What you need
A number of cubes, such as children's building blocks; sticky labels; a board and writing materials; paper; pens and pencils; atlases or maps.

What to do
● Stick labels on each side of several cubes with a lower case letter of the alphabet written on each label. Ensure that the alphabet in capital letters is clearly visible on the wall, should the children need to refer to it.
● Sit the children in groups with writing materials and let them take it in turns to roll one of the cubes. Ask them all to write the capital version of the lower case letter that lands face up.
● When teaching the days of the week and months of the year, you will need to prepare two cubes with the letters *m*, *t*, *w*, *f*, *s*, *j*, *a*, *o*, *n* and *d* on (duplicate the *s* and *m* to cover the 12 sides). Roll a cube and ask the class for either a month of the year or a day of the week (depending on the letter) with a capital letter to start the word. They can write this down and hold it up when they have finished. This will enable you to quickly glance round and check for capital letters and spelling.
● When the children are learning to use capital letters for names, prepare a set of cubes with all the letters of the alphabet on in lower case (if you can leave out two letters, perhaps *X* and *Q*, this would use four cubes). Roll a cube and ask the class to write down a boy or girl's name beginning with that letter, using a capital letter to start the name.
● For place names, the children can work in groups with an atlas or map and a target of 20 places to find.

Differentiation
Less able children can concentrate on learning capital letters, days of the week and names, whereas more able children could use atlases to find place names.

AGE RANGE 5–6

LEARNING OBJECTIVE
To use capital letters for the personal pronoun *I* and for names.

CURRICULUM LINKS
NLS: Year 1, Terms 1 and 2

Who am I?

What you need

A board and writing materials; large cards with the names of class members on them, book characters and cartoon characters written on them; individual whiteboards or paper; pens.

What to do

● Begin by writing a huge capital *I* on the board with a lower case *i* beside it. Explain to the children that because each one of them is important, they must use a capital letter when they use I to talk about themselves.

● Ask them to write a big I on their whiteboard or a piece of paper, and hold it up when they are ready to tell the class something about themselves. For example, *I can ride a bike*. Get them to place emphasis on the pronoun.

● Tell the class that they are going to play a game called 'Who am I?'. Show them the name cards. Explain that the person at the front will pretend to be the person on the card and will describe themselves using sentences beginning with the pronoun I. (Decide whether you wish to introduce the term pronoun at this stage.) The class has to then guess who they are.

● Describe the first character yourself to show the children what to do. To reinforce the objective of the lesson, write each sentence on the board with emphasis on the capital *I*. For example, *I like to walk in the woods, I am nosy, I like eating porridge, I have long blonde hair*. Tell the children they should put up their hands when they are ready to have a guess. They should guess that this is Goldilocks.

● Ask for a volunteer and give them a card. Emphasise that they must only say kind things when describing members of the class. If there is the potential for offence, avoid using certain names and take care when allocating the cards to volunteers.

● As the children describe their characters, write their sentences on the board. Ensure that they begin with I. When the correct name is given write it on the board, emphasising that names need capital letters too.

Differentiation

More able children could write a description of themselves, or as if they were a character, with each sentence beginning with I. Less able children could work in a group and write a collective description of an agreed character, with adult assistance.

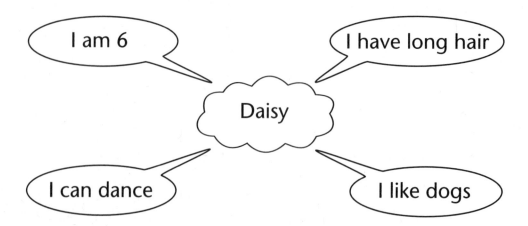

AGE RANGE 7–8

LEARNING OBJECTIVE
To recognise that a noun can be singular or plural, and to be able to convert one to the other.

CURRICULUM LINKS
NLS: Year 3, Term 2

The plurals game

What you need
A set of rule cards (photocopiable page 30), photocopied onto card and cut up, for each group of three children; a set of noun cards (photocopiable page 31), photocopied onto card and cut up, for each group; individual whiteboards or paper; pens.

What to do
● This game can be played once the class understands the meaning of singular and plural, and when the rules for converting nouns into the plural form have been taught. Use the rule cards on photocopiable page 30 if appropriate.
● Put the children into groups of three. They will take turns to be the scorer, the player and the question master. Each group should have a set of rule cards on the table in front of them.
● The question master should have a set of five noun cards, which they keep hidden. Their job is to read the singular noun on the card to the player, who will get one point for choosing the correct rule for converting it to the plural form and one point for spelling the correct plural version of the noun. These should both be written on a whiteboard or piece of paper. The question master may write the singular form of the noun on their whiteboard if the player would like this. If the singular noun on the card was *puppy*, the player would get one point for writing 'Rule 2' and a second point for spelling *puppies*.
● The scorer acts as referee and keeps score on their whiteboard.
● After the five cards have been read out and the total score added up, the children swap around until each child has taken on each role. A different set of five cards should be used for each player.
● At the end of the game the class can compare scores. The game can be played again with different sets of noun cards.

Differentiation
● The rules on the rule cards may be introduced in stages depending on the ability of the class. Alternatively, introduce all the rules during the whole class sessions, but group the children according to ability and assign them an appropriate number of rules. For example, more able children may use all seven, whereas less able children may use just two rules.
● The noun cards should also be allocated according to ability. If a group is only using rule cards 1 and 2, only the noun cards that accompany rules 1 and 2 should be used.

AGE RANGE 8–9

LEARNING OBJECTIVE
To identify adverbs and collect and classify examples.

CURRICULUM LINKS
NLS: Year 4, Term 1

The 'tell us' trees

What you need
A display board; a board and writing materials; a large number of leaf shapes cut out of different autumnal coloured card; black marker pens.

What to do
● Before the lesson, prepare a display board with three large trees drawn on it. Give each tree one of the following labels: *The 'tell us how' tree, The 'tell us when' tree, The 'tell us where' tree.*
● Introduce adverbs to the class. Explain that there are different categories of adverbs – adverbs which tell us 'how' something is done (*happily, noisily*), adverbs which tell us 'when' something is done (*daily, later, soon*) and adverbs which tell us 'where' something is done (*here, near, there*). Explain that these are adverbs of manner, time and place.
● Ask the children questions that lead them to give answers containing adverbs. For example, *How should you clean your teeth? (Carefully.) How would you greet the Queen? (Politely.).* List the adverbs that arise from these questions on the board.
● Introduce the 'tell us' trees and the leaf shapes to the children. Explain that you want them to collect adverbs, write them on the leaves and stick them onto the correct tree. Demonstrate this by adding several leaves with adverbs written on to each tree to get the display started.
● The children should use their reading books to search for adverbs. They can discuss their work at home too, and bring in examples.
● The display should be added to over the coming days or weeks. When the trees are full, carry out a follow-up lesson to discuss what has been achieved. Ask the children to select their favourite adverbs and to write sentences containing these words.

Differentiation
For less able children, during the follow-up lesson write a number of questions and provide a selection of adverbs for them to choose from for their answers. More able children should write imaginative sentences containing the adverbs they find on strips of brown paper. The strips can be used to create fencing beside the trees on the display.

Grammar and
Punctuation
Lifesavers

BRIGHT
IDEAS

AGE RANGE 8–9

LEARNING OBJECTIVE
To investigate the effects of substituting adverbs in clauses or sentences.

CURRICULUM LINKS
NLS: Year 4, Term 1

How did they do it?

What you need
Photocopiable page 32; a board and writing materials; pens.

What to do
● Explain to the children that one of the functions of an adverb is to tell us 'how' something is done and that the adverbs that tell us this often end in -ly.

● Demonstrate this by writing the date on the board very slowly. Ask the children what you are doing (*writing the date*). Then ask how you are doing it (*slowly*). Explain that slowly is the adverb. Provide other examples, such as speaking quietly, shouting loudly.

● When you are sure that the children understand the concept, encourage them to suggest further examples. List these on the board until there is a bank of approximately 20 different adverbs.

● Ensure that the children understand the meaning of all the words.

● Put the children in pairs and give each pair a copy of photocopiable page 32. Give the children a set time in which to choose an adverb for each sentence and give a reason why the subject carried out the action in that manner. They may use adverbs from the list on the board or use their own ideas. Do the first sentence together to stimulate their imaginations and to reiterate the fact that an adverb can have a marked impact on the meaning of the sentence. For example, *Daniel got out of bed slowly because today he had an exam and he did not want to go to school!* is very different to, *Daniel got out of bed excitedly because today was the first day of the holidays and he had so much to look forward to!* Encourage the children to be inventive with their answers.

● After the set time is up, ask the children to compare their choices and reasonings with the rest of the class.

● All the sentences, with the exception of number 12, begin with the subject. Let the children experiment with re-ordering the sentences and moving the adverb. Does this affect the meaning of the sentence and are there any implications for punctuation? Which sentence structure do they think is more effective?

Differentiation
More able children should not restrict themselves to the adverb selection on the board. Encourage them to use a dictionary and thesaurus to locate new and imaginative adverbs. Less able children could work in a group with adult supervision, discussing the reasons for the choices they make.

AGE RANGE 9–11

LEARNING OBJECTIVE
To identify, classify and use a range of prepositions.

CURRICULUM LINKS
NLS: Year 5, Term 3

Up and over

What you need
A soft toy; a board and writing materials; paper; drawing materials.

What to do
● Introduce the term *preposition* to the children. Explain that it is a word that describes the relationship between two nouns. Explain that prepositions can indicate position (*on the table*), direction (*to school*), means (*on foot*), accompaniment (*with a friend*) and time (*after school*).

● Use a soft toy to encourage the children to come up with a range of prepositions of position and direction. Ask, Where is the teddy? as you place the toy in different positions. Write the prepositions suggested on the board. Make sure that you include the following words: *on, above, under, over, through, beneath, in, by, beside, beyond, between, up, down, left, right, past, along, at, into.*

● Give each child a piece of paper and drawing materials and explain that you are going to give them instructions for creating a drawing. The instructions will use prepositions to indicate where they should draw each feature.

● When everyone is listening carefully, begin your instructions. You may wish to write each instruction on the board, using capitals or a different colour for the prepositions. For example:
    – draw a small square **in** the centre of the page
    – put a triangle **on** top of the square
    – **inside** the square, draw a flower
    – write your name **above** the triangle.

● Ask the children to compare their drawings to see if the results were similar – this will probably cause some amusement!

● Follow this up by asking the children to describe the relationship between two of the features in their drawings. For example, *The flower is beneath the triangle.* Ask them to confirm which preposition they used in their sentence.

● Finish by asking the children to make a drawing themselves, using a number of shapes in different positions. Tell them to keep their drawing hidden. Then, with a partner, they can take it in turns to give instructions using prepositions, so that their partner can replicate their drawing. When their partner has finished, the two drawings can be compared to see if the items have been drawn in the correct positions.

Differentiation
Less able children could work in a group with a learning support assistant and use 2-D shapes to construct their pictures. More able children may like to incorporate different colours in their instructions when working in pairs. For example, *Draw a square with the red pencil.*

Grammar and
Punctuation
Lifesavers

AGE RANGE 9–11

LEARNING OBJECTIVE
To identify, classify and use a range of prepositions.

CURRICULUM LINKS
NLS: Year 5, Term 3

Journey time

What you need
Stories with maps in them, such as *Winnie the Pooh* by AA Milne (Egmont), *A Busy Day for a Good Grandmother* by Margaret Mahy (Puffin) or *Little Wolf's Book of Badness* by Ian Whybrow (HarperCollins); PE equipment, such as mats, benches, ropes, hoops, beams, cones; cards with prepositions on them.

What to do
● Use the maps in the story books to discuss the journeys that the characters make with the children. Ask the children to identify the prepositions they use when describing the characters' journeys. Explain that these prepositions indicate direction.
● Tell the children they are going to make journeys of their own whilst thinking about prepositions. Take the class into the hall and set up the PE equipment randomly. Allocate a Start and Finish point.
● Sit the class together in pairs at one side of the hall with the preposition cards set out in front of them.
● Choose a pair to begin. Explain to the children that Child A will give directions and Child B will follow the directions. Tell them that the aim is for Child A to direct Child B from the Start to the Finish in one minute, using as many prepositions as they can in their directions.
● As each preposition is used, for example, walk along the beam, crawl under the bench, Child A can collect the corresponding preposition card. When the minute is up the points can be totalled. Devise a scoring system that will be good practice for times tables, for example, each card gets three points.
● Keep a record of the score for each pair and note the more inventive use of prepositions and verbs.

Differentiation
When carrying out the activity in the hall, let the more able children go first. This will allow the less able children to learn from them.

AGE RANGE 7–11

LEARNING OBJECTIVE
To learn how sentences can be joined in more complex ways using a widening range of conjunctions.

CURRICULUM LINKS
NLS: Year 3, Term 3; Year 6, Term 1

I've started, so you finish!

What you need
A board; photocopiable page 33, one for each team of four; pens.

What to do
● Ensure the children know that conjunctions are words that join two clauses within a sentence and that they can affect the meaning of the sentence.
● Brainstorm a list of conjunctions with the children, writing the conjunctions from page 33 on the board as each one is suggested.
● Put the children into teams of about four, giving each team a copy of page 33. Allocate one child to be the scribe.
● Explain to the children that you are going to give them a starting clause and they must choose a conjunction from the board and then complete the sentence.
● Read out the first sentence starter and set a time limit for each team to complete the sentence on the photocopiable.
● Then move around the room and look at the sentences the teams have created. Allocate points for sentences that make sense and extra points for imaginative work.
● Work through the sentence starters in this way and keep a record of the scores on the board.
● Follow this up by giving each child sentence starters and letting them complete the sentences in their own time.

Differentiation
For less able children, give out sentence starters, endings and conjunctions on strips of card so that they can construct sentences on the table in front of them before writing them down. You may also like to put the sentence starters on one coloured card and the endings on another.

More able children could experiment with using conjunctions at the beginning of a sentence and separating the two clauses with a comma. For example, *Although it was raining, we went out to play.*

It was a lovely sunny day so they went to play in the park...

Grammar and Punctuation Lifesavers

BRIGHT IDEAS

AGE RANGE 8–11

LEARNING OBJECTIVE
To learn how to use connectives to structure an argument.

CURRICULUM LINKS
NLS: Year 4, Term 3; Year 5, Term 3

Points of view

What you need
A board and writing materials; large strips of sugar paper (enough for five for each group); marker pens.

What to do
● Ensure that the children understand that connectives are words or phrases which link sentences together, joining ideas so that they flow and give meaning to the writing. Explain that connectives do this by:
 1. adding together similar points (*moreover, also, furthermore*)
 2. contrasting two different points (*however, on the other hand*)
 3. explaining a point (*for example, in other words*)
 4. forming a list of points (*firstly, finally*)
 5. indicating the outcome (*therefore, consequently, in conclusion*).
Write these five points on the board for the children to see and refer to later.

● Ask the children if they have ever had an argument! Discuss what the arguments were about and highlight that an argument usually occurs because there are two different opinions. Explain that in order to win an argument, they would need to be able to put their point of view across in a convincing way and that connectives can help them to do this more effectively.

● Discuss topical issues relevant to your area, or create a fictitious issue to turn into an argument, such as the sale of the school sports field for a housing development.

● Ask the class to think of all the points for and against the argument, and list these on the board.

● Put the children into small groups of those who are for the argument and those who are against it. Hand out five strips of paper and pens to each group. Tell the children that for each of the five types of connective on the board, they should come up with their own sentence for or against the argument.
Stress that they must use a connective to structure their argument each time. They should write each sentence onto one of their strips of paper.

● Read each group's sentences and discuss how convincing they are. Take the best sentences from each group to construct two class points of view – one for and one against the argument.

Differentiation
For less able children, write a number of sentences onto strips of paper (use one colour for points for, and another colour for points against) and provide the connectives on cards. Help them to choose points to join together and select connectives to help them do this. More able children should construct the whole argument and present it as a letter to a relevant person.

AGE RANGE 7–8

LEARNING OBJECTIVE
To identify pronouns, and distinguish between personal and possessive pronouns.

CURRICULUM LINKS
NLS: Year 3, Term 3

Identikit

What you need
A board and writing materials; paper; acetate sheets; an OHP; highlighter pens.

What to do
● Explain to the children that a pronoun is a word that takes the place of a noun and that its job is to stop us from repeating the same noun over and over again when we are writing. Give an example: _Tom played football on Saturday and Tom scored the winning goal_. Ask the children what they could replace _Tom_ with the second time it appears – _he_. Explain that _he_ is a personal pronoun. Make a list of common personal pronouns on the board. For example, _I, me, we, us_ (first person); _you_ (second person); _he, him, she, her, it, they, them_ (third person).
● Explain that we use possessive pronouns to tell us who something belongs to and make a list of these on the board. For example, _my, mine_ (first person); _your, yours_ (second person); _his, hers, its, ours, theirs_ (third person).
● Explain to the children that they are going to write a personal profile of themselves using first person personal and possessive pronouns. Ask if anyone knows which these are? (_I, me, we, us, my, mine_.)
● Write a list of things they should include on the board, such as height, hair colour, eyes, favourite sport, hobbies. Write the first sentences together. For example, _I am very tall for my age. I have long red hair. My eyes are green. My family lives in a cottage._
● Collect the children's work in and select several good examples to copy onto acetate – if necessary, word process the work for clarity.
● At the beginning of the next session, recap the lists of personal and possessive pronouns. Then project one of the profiles onto a whiteboard. Ask a volunteer to come and highlight all the pronouns. The class can help out.
● Ask volunteers to change the pronoun from the first to the third person. For example, _I am tall_ would become _He is tall_. The profile can then be read out again and the class can guess the child's identity.
● Another volunteer can change the pronoun into the second person, to tell the child what they said about themselves. For example, _You are tall_.

Differentiation
For less able children, write out a structure for them to complete with appropriate pronouns. More able children could write their profile in the third person.

Grammar and
Punctuation
Lifesavers

BRIGHT IDEAS

AGE RANGE 7–8

LEARNING OBJECTIVE
To use the past tense consistently for narration.

CURRICULUM LINKS
NLS: Year 3, Term 1

Are you sitting comfortably?

What you need
Cards to write on; props for acting out the story; a board and writing materials.

What to do
● Before the lesson, choose a well-known story, such as a traditional fairy story or a picture book known to the class, that can be easily broken down into clear stages. Prepare a card for each stage of the story, outlining the action that takes place.
● Choose the required number of children to play the characters in the story. Tell them that you want them to mime the action described on the cards. You might like to help them prepare this before the lesson and prepare props to help them act out the action.
● At the beginning of the lesson, tell the class that the actors are going to act out a well-known story. Tell them what the title of the story is and which character each child will be playing.
● Let the actors mime the action on the first card. Ask the rest of the class to describe what is happening. On the board, write up the scene in the present tense. For example, *Scene 1: The Three Billy Goats Gruff are grazing in a field. They are dreaming about the lovely green grass they can see on the other side of the river.*
● When the whole story has been acted out, explain that this version of the story is written in the present tense, as if it is happening now, rather like a sports commentary.
● Explain that when we write or tell stories we usually use the past tense, because we are telling the listener about something that has already happened.
● As a class, highlight all the verbs used in the present tense version.
● Next, ask the children to help you convert all the verbs into the past tense. For example: *Scene 1: The Three Billy Goats Gruff were grazing in a field. They dreamt about the lovely green grass they could see on the other side of the river.*
● Re-read the new version of the story slowly, allowing the actors to carry out their mime again.
● To follow this up, the children could write up the story in the past tense, underlining the verbs.

Differentiation
Write out the story for less able children, leaving gaps for the verbs. More able children could choose a different story and summarise the story in stages in both the present and past tense – highlighting the verbs they have used in both cases.

AGE RANGE 6–9

LEARNING OBJECTIVE
To learn the function of verbs in sentences by collecting and classifying examples of verbs from own knowledge.

CURRICULUM LINKS
NLS: Year 2, Term 2; Year 3, Term 1; Year 4, Term 1

What can you do?

What you need
A board and writing materials; a number of balls (enough for one per pair); a hall or outdoor space; a selection of different sized balls; tubes of card; labels; circles of brightly-coloured card; pens.

What to do
● Whilst writing *verb* on the board, ask the class what you are doing. Confirm that you are writing. Explain that *to write* is a verb and that verbs are a special group of words which explain an action, or a state of being.
● Mime other actions for the class to guess, and encourage them to name the root verb, such as *to laugh* or *to cry*. Write these examples on the board.
● When you feel they understand the concept of a verb ask each child to give you an example of a root verb. Tell them to pass if they can't think of one.

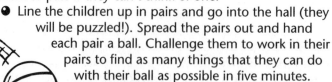

● Line the children up in pairs and go into the hall (they will be puzzled!). Spread the pairs out and hand each pair a ball. Challenge them to work in their pairs to find as many things that they can do with their ball as possible in five minutes.
● Start the timer and circulate, checking that the children are on task.
● After five minutes, stop the activity, collect the balls and ask each pair to tell you one thing they did with their ball. Tell them you want their answers in sentences, for example *I threw my ball*. Ask the children to identify the verb in their sentence (*to throw*).
● Back in the classroom, record the selection of verbs the children found, such as *to roll, to drop, to bounce, to juggle*, in sentences on the board.
● A selection of different sized balls with the root verbs stuck on as labels could be used to make a small display. Balance the balls on tubes of card. The children could write up what they did onto bright card circles to display behind the balls. For example, *I threw my ball*.

Differentiation
Challenge more able children to collect as many verbs as they can think of related to sport and put them into sentences. Provide assistance for less able children when writing up what they did onto their card circles.

Grammar and Punctuation Lifesavers

AGE RANGE 8–9

LEARNING OBJECTIVE
To identify and use powerful verbs to enhance text level work.

CURRICULUM LINKS
NLS: Year 4, Term 1

Up, up and away!

What you need
Brightly-coloured card; brown card; string; sticky tape; thesauruses, one per group; text extracts containing examples of powerful verbs that relate to those you wish the class to investigate, one per group; large sheets of paper; pens.

What to do
● Before the lesson, prepare hot air balloons for displaying your findings. Cut out two balloon shapes in brightly-coloured card, and two baskets from brown card. Attach the strings, which will connect the basket and the balloon, using sticky tape. Then glue the second balloon and basket shapes on top of the first, in order to hide the sticky tape. Attach a thread from the top of the balloon to suspend it from the ceiling.
● On each basket write a common verb that you want the children to investigate. For example, *to eat, to go, to look*. Write the verb on both sides of the basket so that it will be seen from all angles when suspended.
● Put the class into small groups and explain that they are going to make a collection of powerful verbs to use as a reference for their written work. Explain how the use of powerful verbs conveys stronger images and that a piece of writing can be brought to life when using them. Give an example: *The tramp ate the burger* could become *The tramp hungrily devoured the burger*. Give them other examples using common verbs and encourage them to give more imaginative suggestions.
● Draw a mind map on the board for each verb on the balloons (see below). Give each group a large piece of paper and pens, a thesaurus and text extracts. Ask them to copy the mind maps onto the paper. Explain that they should search for powerful verbs for each of those on the mind maps, using the thesaurus and text extracts, and record as many as they can find.

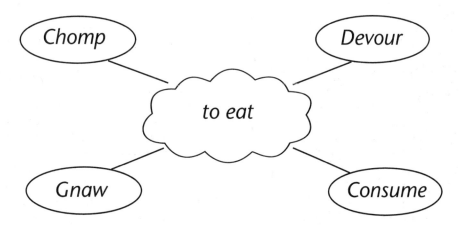

● Set a time limit for the groups. At the end of this time, collect their findings on the board (there will be duplications).
● When the class have agreed on the best ones, these can be written onto each balloon. The balloons can be suspended from the ceiling and used as a reference point during the children's writing.

Differentiation
Less able children can focus on one common verb and use a simple thesaurus. More able children should use a more advanced thesaurus and text extracts appropriate to their reading ability.

AGE RANGE 8–10

LEARNING OBJECTIVE
To investigate how the future tense is formed using auxiliary verbs.

CURRICULUM LINKS
NLS: Year 4, Term 1; Year 5, Term 1

Sunshine and showers

What you need
A large outline map of the UK; marker pen; weather symbols (weather symbols used in the UK can be found at: www.bbc.co.uk/weather/features/symbols.shtml); atlases; a board and writing materials; photocopiable page 34; pens and coloured pencils.

What to do
● The day before the lesson, ask the children to watch the weather forecast on the television and/or to cut out forecasts from a newspaper. Ask them to make a note of the weather symbols used.
● At the start of the lesson, discuss what they saw or read and whether the forecast was correct. Highlight the fact that the weather forecast is telling us about something that hasn't happened yet – it is given in the future tense.
● Ask for volunteers to read out some sentences from their forecasts and write these on the board. For example, *There is going to be heavy rain in the north*, *The south will be sunny*. Highlight the future tense of the verb and that auxiliary verbs are used with other verbs to form the future tense. These are: *be, have, do, can and will*.
● Put up the outline map of the UK and hand out atlases. Discuss and locate places that the children know on the map. Include their home location, holiday destinations or places where relatives live. Write these on the map and ensure that there is a spread of place names across it.
● Tell the children you want them to help you create a fictitious weather forecast for the UK. Ask them for sentences to describe the weather in the places that are labelled on the map. Remind them to give you sentences in the future tense.
● As they give you their sentences record these on the board and attach the weather symbols to the map in the appropriate locations. Ask for volunteers to highlight the future tense verbs used in their sentences.
● The children can create their own weather forecast using photocopiable page 34. They should underline the future tense verbs that they use in their sentences.

Differentiation
Mark five locations on the map on the photocopiable sheet for less able children. Ask questions to prompt what they think the weather will be like at each location. Write down their sentences for them to copy and help them to locate the verbs. More able children could study the weather forecasts on the Internet before writing more detailed weather reports.

Grammar and
Punctuation
Lifesavers

BRIGHT
IDEAS

AGE RANGE 7–8

LEARNING OBJECTIVE
To understand the differences between verbs in the first, second and third person.

CURRICULUM LINKS
NLS: Year 3, Term 3; Year 5, Term 1

Person to person

What you need
Hall space; a stopwatch.

What to do
● Introduce the distinction between the first, second and third person. Explain that the first person is used when referring to oneself and that the pronouns *I*, *my and we* are used. The second person is used when referring to one's listener and the pronoun *you* is used. The third person is used when referring to somebody else and the pronoun *he*, *she*, *it* or *they* will be used.

● Take the children into the hall and put them into pairs where the individuals do not know each other that well. Each pair should sit facing each other.

● Let the children decide who is to be A and who is to be B. Then explain that A will begin and has one minute to tell B as much as they can about themselves. For example, *My name is Sophie. I am eight years old. I like ballet and rugby…* Explain that B must listen very carefully to what they are being told.

● After the minute is up, stop the pairs and explain that A was speaking in the first person – they were using the pronouns *I*, *my* and *we*.

● Tell the children that it is now B's turn to relate back to A what they have learnt, again in one minute. For example, *Your name is Sophie. You are eight years old. You like ballet and rugby…*

● After a minute stop the children and point out that B has been using the second person. The pairs can then swap over and repeat the process.

● After this, bring the children together in a circle. Ask a volunteer to tell the class about their partner. For example, *Sophie is eight years old. She likes ballet and rugby…* Point out that now the speaker is using the third person.

● To follow this up, the children could write a diary over the weekend which they could swap in class and their partner could write it up in the third person.

Differentiation
For less able children, prepare a diary entry. Highlight all the personal pronouns that will need to be changed in order to turn the text into the third person. Work with these children. More able children could be given a more advanced piece of text for conversion, such as an extract from *Anne Frank's Diary*.

AGE RANGE 8–9

LEARNING OBJECTIVE
To use the apostrophe accurately to show possession.

CURRICULUM LINKS
NLS: Year 4, Term 2

Lost property

What you need
Personal possessions belonging to eight children in the class; a box; a board and writing materials; individual whiteboards and pens; paper; photocopiable page 35.

What to do
● Before the lesson choose eight children from whom you can select personal objects which the class will be able to easily identify their owner from. For example, a child who is known to be keen on tennis may bring in a tennis racket.
● At the beginning of the lesson, sit the eight children at the front of the class and have the objects in a box marked *Lost property*. Explain to the class that you need their help to find the owners of a number of items.
● On the board write the sentence, *The _____ belongs to _____* eight times. Also write the names of the eight children to assist the class with spelling (emphasise the use of capital letters!). Tell the children to copy the sentence on their whiteboards.
● Pull out the first item, confirm what it is and write this in the first space in the first sentence on the board. Encourage the children to complete the sentence and then hold up their whiteboard. For example, *The tennis racket belongs to Siu Yin*. Compare answers and see which children were correct.
● Now explain that an easier way of writing this sentence would be, *It is Siu Yin's tennis racket*. Explain the rules for using the possessive apostrophe with a single or collective noun – the apostrophe comes before the s. Explain that if the name ends in s the apostrophe comes after the s – an extra s is not added.
● Repeat this for the other items in the box.
● After all eight items have been identified, leave the sentences with the names and the items on the board. Give the children some paper and ask them to write up the eight pairs of sentences for themselves. For example, *The scarf belongs to Ben. It is Ben's scarf*.
● Give the children a copy of photocopiable page 35 to complete.

Differentiation
For less able children, put the names of the objects, the children's names, an apostrophe and an s on cards. Write the cloze sentence out for them so that they can make the sentences using the cards and then copy them into their books. Explain to more able children the rule for using possessive apostrophes when there is more than one owner.

My aunt's cat

● Use a dictionary to find an adjective for each letter of the alphabet to describe "My aunt's cat".

A My aunt's cat is an _____ cat

B My aunt's cat is a _____ cat

C My aunt's cat is a _____ cat

D My aunt's cat is a _____ cat

E My aunt's cat is an _____ cat

F My aunt's cat is a _____ cat

G My aunt's cat is a _____ cat

H My aunt's cat is a _____ cat

I My aunt's cat is an _____ cat

J My aunt's cat is a _____ cat

K My aunt's cat is a _____ cat

L My aunt's cat is a _____ cat

M My aunt's cat is a _____ cat

N My aunt's cat is a _____ cat

O My aunt's cat is an _____ cat

P My aunt's cat is a _____ cat

Q My aunt's cat is a _____ cat

R My aunt's cat is a _____ cat

S My aunt's cat is a _____ cat

T My aunt's cat is a _____ cat

U My aunt's cat is an _____ cat

V My aunt's cat is a _____ cat

W My aunt's cat is a _____ cat

X My aunt's cat is a _____ cat

Y My aunt's cat is a _____ cat

Z My aunt's cat is a _____ cat

Mixed bag

Nouns

giraffe	lion	sandwich
troll	dancer	story
night	hedgehog	jumper
trampoline	coin	princess
trainers	mountain	journey
snail	clown	jelly
footpath	teddy bear	bruise
river	glue	castle
joke	teacher	storm

Adjectives

tall	wild	deep
rugged	agile	painful
prickly	long	slimy
fragile	ferocious	ugly
funny	hard	spooky
strict	tasty	fashionable
steep	woolly	dark
sticky	beautiful	funny
shiny	sad	wobbly

Grammar and
Punctuation
Lifesavers

BRIGHT
IDEAS

All together now...

A flock of sheep
A swarm of bees
A pod of whales
A squadron of aeroplanes
A school of dolphins

A bunch of flowers
A crowd of people
A fleet of ships
A herd of cattle
A shoal of fish

A choir of singers
A pack of wolves
A pride of lions
A litter of puppies
A clutch of eggs

The plurals game – rule cards

Rule 1 To make this noun plural I just add an -s.

Rule 2 To make this noun plural I change the -y to -ies.

Rule 3 To make this noun plural I change the -f or -fe to –ves.

Rule 4 To make this noun plural I add -es.
(Hint: use this rule for most nouns ending in -o and for those which make a hissing sound, such as match<u>es</u>.)

Rule 5 I can't change this noun to make it plural because it is always plural.

Rule 6 I don't need to change this noun because it stays the same whether singular or plural.

Rule 7 These are irregular plurals.

Grammar and
Punctuation
Lifesavers

BRIGHT IDEAS

The plurals game – noun cards

table	**Rule 1** tables	potato	**Rule 4** potatoes
chair	**Rule 1** chairs	volcano	**Rule 4** volcanoes
banana	**Rule 1** bananas	tomato	**Rule 4** tomatoes
boy	**Rule 1** boys	match	**Rule 4** matches
girl	**Rule 1** girls	watch	**Rule 4** watches
monkey	**Rule 1** monkeys	trousers	**Rule 5** trousers
party	**Rule 2** parties	shorts	**Rule 5** shorts
baby	**Rule 2** babies	scissors	**Rule 5** scissors
fairy	**Rule 2** fairies	tweezers	**Rule 5** tweezers
puppy	**Rule 2** puppies	sheep	**Rule 6** sheep
story	**Rule 2** stories	deer	**Rule 6** deer
family	**Rule 2** families	fish	**Rule 6** fish
knife	**Rule 3** knives	person	**Rule 7** people
wolf	**Rule 3** wolves	child	**Rule 7** children
loaf	**Rule 3** loaves	man	**Rule 7** men
shelf	**Rule 3** shelves	woman	**Rule 7** women
elf	**Rule 3** elves	mouse	**Rule 7** mice
leaf	**Rule 3** leaves	foot	**Rule 7** feet

How did they do it?

1. Daniel got out of bed _____ because

_____.

2. Daisy walked to school _____ because

_____.

3. Rashid waited for the postman _____ because

_____.

4. Polly ate her dinner _____ because

_____.

5. George opened his presents _____ because

_____.

6. Amy painted a picture _____ because

_____.

7. Milo spoke to the policeman _____ because

_____.

8. Claire cleaned her teeth _____ because

_____.

9. The cat ran _____ because

_____.

10. The old lady sat _____ on the bench because

_____.

12. _____ the mouse scuttled across the floor

_____.

13. The little girl licked her ice cream _____ because

_____.

Grammar and
Punctuation
Lifesavers

BRIGHT IDEAS

I've started, so you finish!

because	but	and	after	since
although	however	or	later	either
if	neither	when	until	nevertheless
so	therefore	before	while	despite

● Complete the sentences with the use of a conjunction.

1. It was a lovely sunny day _____

_____

2. They all decided to go to the park _____

_____

3. The party was wonderful _____

_____

4. Dinosaurs roamed the Earth _____

_____

5. I do not like going to the dentist _____

_____

6. Bobby wasn't allowed to go to the park alone _____

_____

7. Sally played happily with her rabbit _____

_____

8. The film was very frightening _____

_____

9. The boys were sent to bed without any tea _____

_____

10. You must always brush your teeth _____

_____

Sunshine and showers

● Create your own weather symbols
and your own forecast.

Map © Crown copyright

● Write a sentence about the weather in five different places on the map.

1. _____

2. _____

3. _____

4. _____

5. _____

Grammar and
Punctuation
Lifesavers

Lost property

● Match the objects to their owners and complete the sentences.

bridge

Cinderella

Jack

Goldilocks

a troll

Sleeping Beauty

needle

glass slipper

beanstalk

Red Riding Hood

long golden pony tail

basket of goodies

cat

Dick Whittington

1. I think it is _____ _____.

2. I think it is _____ _____.

3. I think it is _____ _____.

4. I think it is _____ _____.

5. I think it is _____ _____.

6. I think it is _____ _____.

7. I think it is _____ _____.

CHAPTER 2

Sentence construction

AGE RANGE 5–8

LEARNING OBJECTIVE
To recognise that a sentence begins with a capital letter and ends with a full stop.

CURRICULUM LINKS
NLS: Year 1, Term 1

Cloud burst sentences

What you need
A whiteboard and pen; white card cut into cloud shapes; shiny blue paper cut into raindrop and puddle shapes; photocopiable page 46; pens.

What to do
● Talk to the children about the weather. Discuss different types of weather, what they can do in different types of weather, and so on. Write down some of the key weather words on the board.
● Next, ask the children:
   1. *Where does rain come from?* (Pin up one of the card clouds on the board.)
   2. *How does rain fall?* (Pin up several shiny raindrop shapes coming down from the cloud.)
   3. *What happens to the rain when it falls?* (Pin a puddle shape underneath the raindrops.)
● Explain to the children that each of the shapes represent a sentence – the cloud represents the beginning, the raindrops signify the middle and the puddle is the end of the sentence.
● Discuss the fact that a sentence begins with a capital letter and ends with a full stop. Tell the children they are each going to create a cloud burst sentence – the first word will go into a cloud, each subsequent word will go into a raindrop and the sentence will end in a puddle!
● Ask the children what will be special about all the words in the clouds (*they will all begin with a capital letter*).
● Ask the children what they will put in the puddle, as it is the end of the sentence (*a full stop*).
● Model several examples, sticking the shapes onto the board. For example, *The* (in a cloud) *sun is hot* (each word in a raindrop) . (full stop in a puddle).
● Hand out a copy of photocopiable page 46 to each child and ask them to think of their own weather sentence, putting the words and punctuation of their sentence into the appropriate shapes.
● The children can use the computer to word process the sentences, which can then be displayed on the prepared clouds, shiny raindrops and puddles.

Differentiation
Differentiation for more able children is likely to be by outcome – they should be encouraged to produce more detailed sentences and will, therefore, need more raindrops. Write out a sentence for less able children and help them to go over the words. Alternatively, write and cut out short sentences for them to arrange and copy.

Grammar and Punctuation Lifesavers

AGE RANGE 7–8

LEARNING OBJECTIVE
To recognise full stops and capital letters when reading and to understand how they affect the way a passage is read; to begin using full stops to demarcate sentences.

CURRICULUM LINKS
NLS: Year 1, Terms 1 and 2

Spot the stop!

What you need
A Big Book; photocopiable page 47, enough for one each and one copied on to acetate; an OHP; coloured pencils.

What to do
● Sit with the children and show them the Big Book. Read the book slowly, making clear stops at each full stop. When you have finished, explain that you are going to read the book again. This time, make a point of not stopping at the full stops, and read it in one breath! Ask the children what was different about the second reading. Establish the function of the full stops and encourage the children to identify them. Read the book again and ask the children to call out when they think you have to take a breath at a full stop.

● Once the function of full stops has been established, put the children into pairs and give each child a copy of photocopiable page 47. Explain to the children that the story consists of nine sentences that need to be identified with full stops and capital letters. Tell them that once they have identified a sentence, it can be written beneath its associated picture on the storyboard.

● Give the children a coloured pencil each and tell them to start by marking where they think a sentence ends and a new one begins in the story.

● Encourage them to read each sentence they find to their partner to check it makes sense, before writing the nine sentences on the storyboard.

● When the children have finished, compare their work and go over the correct answers with the whole class. Use the photocopiable page copied onto acetate and show it on an OHP.

● Follow this up by using a talking book on the computer.

Differentiation
For less able children, write out the sentences for them to copy after they have identified them. Let more able children use the talking books, which will allow them to create their own sentences to go with pictures.

AGE RANGE 6-7

LEARNING OBJECTIVE
To secure the use of simple sentences in their own writing and to write in full sentences.

CURRICULUM LINKS
NLS: Year 2, Term 2; Year 3, Term 1

The subject sack

What you need
A board and writing materials; a Subject Sack – a bag containing a wide variety of items, the more diverse the better (anything from sweets to a picture of the Queen!), ensuring that there are enough items for one each and several to use as examples; pens.

What to do
● Clarify the children's knowledge of what constitutes a sentence. Explain the rules for forming a simple sentence:
1. It has one clause: a clause is something which expresses an event or a situation.
2. A clause has a subject and a verb.
3. The subject is the person or thing in the clause.
4. The verb is the action that is carried out.
● Write a couple of examples on the board, such as *The lion roared* or *A giraffe is a very tall animal*. Underline the subject and verb in each sentence.
● Show the children the Subject Sack. Explain that inside there are lots of items which could be the subject in a sentence.
● Ask for a volunteer to pick something out. Confirm that this is the subject of the sentence and write it on the board.
● Ask the volunteer to give you a simple sentence with the item as the subject. For example, *The Queen is an important lady*. Write this on the board and ask them to identify the verb in their sentence – *is*. Underline both the subject and the verb.
● Let another volunteer choose a subject and then use it to create a simple sentence. Write this on the board, underlining the subject and verb.
● Once the class understand the meaning of a simple sentence, allow them to pick one subject each from the sack. They can then create their own sentence in their books. Tell them to ensure they use a capital letter, full stop (or question mark or exclamation mark) and to underline the subject in red and the verb in blue.
● When they have done this, they should swap subjects with a neighbour and create another sentence in the same way.

Differentiation
Less able children can work in a group with an adult scribing their suggestions and guiding them when identifying the subject and verb. More able children may also identify other parts of speech, as appropriate to their ability.

Grammar and
Punctuation
Lifesavers

BRIGHT
IDEAS

AGE RANGE 9–11

LEARNING OBJECTIVE
To explore ambiguities that arise from sentence contractions.

CURRICULUM LINKS
NLS: Year 5, Term 2

Double trouble

What you need

A variety of newspaper headlines; a board and writing materials; photocopiable page 48 copied onto card and cut up into individual headlines, enough for one set per group; large sheets of paper; marker pens; a computer.

What to do

● Lead into the lesson by discussing newspapers – how they are set out, how articles are written and how journalists draw you into reading an article with catchy headlines.

● Show the children a selection of carefully chosen headlines. Explain that headlines are usually created by shortening a full sentence. Tell them that certain words are missed out for effect, but this can result in an ambiguous statement.

● Write the classic example on the board: *Police shot man with knife*. Ask the class what they think this headline means and point out that it could have a completely different meaning to what was intended. Ask them to expand the headline so that it is unambiguous: *The police shot a man who was carrying a knife*.

● Put the children into groups and provide each group with a set of headlines from photocopiable page 48. For each headline, ask the groups to:

1. Discuss what they think the intended meaning is.
2. Discuss how the headline could be interpreted.
3. Write out the headline so that the meaning is unambiguous.

● Before setting the children to work, discuss the meaning of any difficult words in the headlines, such as vaccine, rabies or truant.

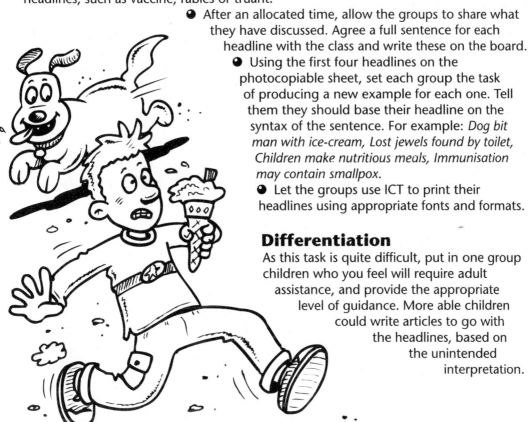

● After an allocated time, allow the groups to share what they have discussed. Agree a full sentence for each headline with the class and write these on the board.

● Using the first four headlines on the photocopiable sheet, set each group the task of producing a new example for each one. Tell them they should base their headline on the syntax of the sentence. For example: *Dog bit man with ice-cream, Lost jewels found by toilet, Children make nutritious meals, Immunisation may contain smallpox.*

● Let the groups use ICT to print their headlines using appropriate fonts and formats.

Differentiation

As this task is quite difficult, put in one group children who you feel will require adult assistance, and provide the appropriate level of guidance. More able children could write articles to go with the headlines, based on the unintended interpretation.

AGE RANGE 9–11

LEARNING OBJECTIVE
To understand the three types of sentence; to investigate clauses through identifying the main clause in a long sentence.

CURRICULUM LINKS
NLS: Year 5, Term 3

Complex definitions

What you need
The definition cards on photocopiable pages 49 and 50 cut out, enough for one set per child; a board and writing materials; paper; pens and coloured pencils.

What to do
● Give each child a set of definition cards. Use them as a stimulus for revising, clarifying and/or introducing the following terms:
1. simple sentence, compound sentence, complex sentence
2. clause, subject, verb, complement, object
3. main clause, subordinate clause.
● Write a variety of different types of sentences on the board. For example:
1. *The lion roared at the trainer.* (Simple sentence.)
2. *Tommy shouted loudly.* (Simple sentence.)
3. *Claire went to ballet and Amy did her homework.* (Compound sentence.)
4. *The rabbit ate lettuce and the guinea pig munched on a carrot.* (Compound sentence.)
5. *The teacher, who had a terrible headache, sighed as she entered the classroom.* (Complex sentence.)
6. *Although she found science difficult, she was determined to pass her exams.* (Complex sentence.)
● Ask the children to hold up the card that correctly identifies each sentence type as you write it on the board.
● Next, underline different parts of each sentence and ask the children to identify the main clause, subordinate clause, subject, object, verb and complement.
● Create a colour coded key, for example, *main clause = blue, subordinate clause = red*. Write a set of sentences on the board. Ask the children to copy out and identify the type of sentence, and finally to use the appropriate colours to underline and label the different parts of the sentence.

Differentiation
Less able children can focus on identifying the main clause only. More able children could then go on to create their own examples of each type of sentence, again using the colour coded key to identify the parts of each sentence.

AGE RANGE 9–11

Learning objective
To learn how to construct complex sentences to enhance their own writing.

Curriculum links
NLS: Year 6, Term 1

Complex creations

What you need
A board and different coloured writing materials; photocopiable page 51; pens; popular texts where both simple and complex sentences have been used.

What to do
● Go through a definition of complex sentences with the children:
1. They have a main clause and at least one subordinate clause.
2. The main clause can stand alone.
3. The subordinate clause cannot stand alone.
4. Connectives can be used to join the clauses together.
5. The connectives can be placed in the middle of the sentence or at the beginning.
6. Extra clauses can be dropped into the main clause and punctuated with commas.

● Write a complex sentence on the board. For example, _Although the snow lay thick on the ground and the wind was bitter,_ **Tommy would not turn back** _until he had found his little dog_. With the children, identify the main clause (shown here in bold) and underline it in red, and the subordinate clauses (shown here underlined) and underline them in blue.

● Confirm the number of clauses in the sentence (four), then ask the children to try and separate them into simple sentences. For example:
1. _The snow lay thick on the ground._
2. _The wind was bitter._
3. _Tommy would not turn back._
4. _He had to find his little dog._

● Discuss with the children how these four clauses have been joined using connectives at both the start and in the middle of the sentence. Ask the children to locate these and circle them in green.
● Repeat with a sentence where the subordinate clause has been dropped into the main clause. For example, _Tommy, who was searching for his little dog, trudged through the thick snow._
● Give the children a copy of photocopiable page 51 and let them work through the sheet independently.
● Explain to the children that while simple sentences give one piece of information and can grab the reader's attention, complex sentences add interest as they contain more than one piece of information and can be used to contrast different ideas. Read some of the texts with the children and discuss how these sentences are used.

Differentiation
More able children could search for examples of complex sentences in books. Let them identify the main and subordinate clauses, change the clauses into simple sentences and identify how the clauses were joined to form a complex sentence. Provide support for less able children when working on the photocopiable sheet.

AGE RANGE 9–11

Learning objective
To secure control of complex sentences, understanding how clauses can be used to achieve different effects.

Curriculum links
NLS: Year 6, Terms 2 and 3

Scene setting

What you need
Four or five text extracts (enough for one per group of three) where both simple and complex sentences have been used to describe the story setting, for example *The Wolves of Willoughby Chase* (Red Fox) and *Midnight is a Place* (Hodder) by Joan Aiken.

What to do
● Recap the rules for creating complex sentences. Write a number of examples of complex sentences on the board, highlighting how they have been formed.
● Put the children into twos or threes and hand out the text extracts. Allow the children some time for reading and analysis. Tell them they should identify the simple and complex sentences. Tell them you also want them to look at how the complex sentences have been formed and why the author may have chosen to write the sentence in this way.
● Discuss each group's findings as a class.
● Next, write a list of different settings on the board. These could be a scrap yard, the edge of the ocean, a deserted building and a busy city centre. Tell the children you want them to spend ten minutes picturing one of the settings in their 'mind's eye'. Explain that they should write down ideas to include in an atmospheric description of the setting.
● The children can then work in groups, according to which setting they chose. Explain that you want them to pool their ideas in their groups and use them to create a story setting.
● Tell the children that you want them to learn how to use complex sentences and to use clauses to create different effects in their story settings. Suggest they create a list of separate ideas and then experiment with combining them into complex sentences. Explain that it is a good idea to start with a main clause and decide which other information to bring into the sentence. Tell them they should consider whether they wish to make a contrast, or give extra detail in their description.
● The completed story settings could be used as the basis for a piece of artwork. The two could then be displayed alongside one another.

Differentiation
Provide less able children with the details you wish them to incorporate into each sentence and suggest connectives they could use. More able children could model their sentences on complex sentences from advanced texts.

Grammar and
Punctuation
Lifesavers

BRIGHT
IDEAS

AGE RANGE 8–9

Learning objective
To understand the significance of word order; to understand that by re-ordering some sentences the meaning can be destroyed, whilst by re-ordering others the meaning can be retained.

Curriculum links
NLS: Year 4, Term 2

Order, order!

What you need
Photocopiable page 52, the sentences cut up into individual words (enough for the children to work in small groups with each group having all the sentences); envelopes (one for each cut up sentence); paper; pens.

What to do
● Before the lesson, place each cut-up sentence from photocopiable page 52 into its own envelope. Number the envelopes according to the number of each sentence on the photocopiable sheet.

● Start the lesson by explaining to the children that the order in which we place words in a sentence can affect its meaning. Explain that if you re-order the words, the sentence may still make sense, but it may have a different meaning. Explain that sometimes, however, the words can be re-ordered and the sentence will still mean the same in both cases.

● Put the children into small groups and hand each group a set of envelopes.

● Ask the groups to open 'Envelope 1' and to look at the words inside it. Explain that the aim is to take one envelope at a time – important so that the words are not muddled up! – and arrange the words into a sentence that makes sense. Tell them they should then check to see if there is more than one way in which the words can be ordered. It is possible that they can make a second sentence that has the same meaning as the first, or one that means something else. Tell them to write down the sentences they make, numbering them with the same number as was on the envelope.

● When the groups have finished, compare their findings as a class. Discuss why the word order is important according to the rules below:

    1. The subject usually precedes the verb, otherwise the meaning is changed. (Sentences 1, 2 and 3.)

    2. The order of words in a noun phrase is not flexible. (Sentences 4, 5 and 6.)

    3. Some adverbial phrases can be moved. (Sentences 7 and 8.)

    4. Some prepositional phrases can be moved. (Sentences (9 and 10.)

Differentiation
Put the children into mixed ability groups. More able children could create their own sentences that follow the rules for word order.

AGE RANGE 10–11

Learning objective
To explore the use of conditionals in deduction, speculation and supposition.

Curriculum links
NLS: Year 6, Term 2

If...

What you need
A board and writing materials; a copy of 'If' by Rudyard Kipling copied onto acetate; OHP and pens; paper; pens.

What to do
● Hold a discussion with the children. Ask if they have ever asked their parents or carers for something and the response has been, On one condition… or If… For example, *If you finish your homework, you can go to the park.*
● Explain that such sentences are known as conditionals, where one thing depends on another. These sentences may contain one of these conjunctions: *if, unless, providing, as long as.*
● A common conditional sentence that people often use regards the lottery. Ask the children if they have ever heard adults say what they would do if they won the lottery. Ask them what they would do themselves. Write up some of the examples on the board and highlight the conjunctions and punctuation.
● Follow this light-hearted introduction to conditionals by introducing the children to one of the longest and most famous conditional sentences – 'If' by Rudyard Kipling.
● Display the poem on the OHP and take each condition one at a time, asking the children if they understand what is meant by it. Explain that in essence the poem is explaining what it takes to be a good person.
● After analysing the poem with the children, brainstorm a list of adjectives to describe personality traits. For example, *brave, daring, confident, creative, caring, generous, honest, loving, kind, humorous.*
● Ask the children to work in pairs to create conditional sentences similar to those in the poem. Tell them to think of examples of what a person might do in order to be attributed with different personality traits. For example, *If you walked a tightrope across a raging river, you would be a daring person.*
● Let the class share their contributions and then combine the best examples to create a class version of 'If'.

Differentiation
More able children could work in a group to analyse Rudyard Kipling's poem before the lesson in order to contribute their findings during the analysis. Less able children could create scenarios and choose which adjectives describe what characters would be like.

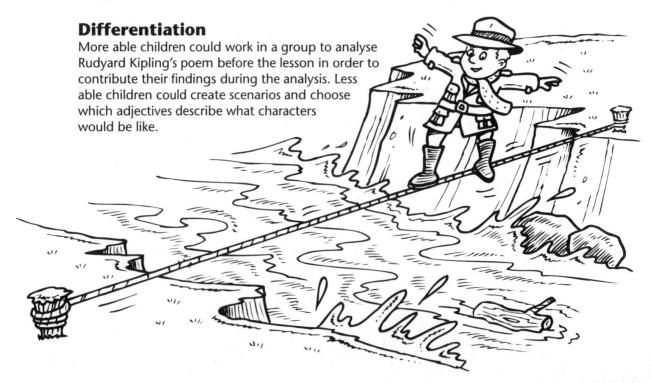

AGE RANGE 7–9

Learning objective
To learn how to use words or phrases to signal time sequences.

Curriculum links
NLS: Year 3, Term 3

It happened like this...

What you need
A board and writing materials; a video player; television; two cartoons, such as Tom and Jerry or Bugs Bunny; paper; pens.

What to do
● Discuss with the children the concept of time phrases – words we use to indicate the order in which things happen. Explain that these are used in particular when giving instructions, when recounting an event and in stories.
● Brainstorm some time phrases and write them up on the board in three groups – beginning, middle and end time phrases. For example, beginning time phrases: *firstly, first, in the beginning, at the start, one day*; middle time phrases: *then, later on, after, next, soon, when, in between, secondly, while, afterwards, until*; end time phrases: *finally, in the end, in conclusion, lastly*.
● Explain to the children that they are going to watch a short cartoon. Tell them they must watch carefully, as afterwards they are going to recount the events that happened – in the correct order!
● Let the children watch the cartoon. Afterwards, ask for a volunteer to recount what happened in the story. Tell the other children to listen out for time phrases that are used and to put their hands up every time they hear one. It is likely that *and then* will be used quite frequently!
● After this first attempt, ask the children to recount what happened again, asking for one sentence at a time. Tell the children to choose a time phrase for their sentence from the board before volunteering.
● As each sentence is given and agreed, write it up on the board to create a narrative for the cartoon.
● Watch the cartoon again, stopping and starting at the appropriate points to check whether the recount of what happened is in the correct order.
● To follow this up, let the children watch a second cartoon for which they have to write their own recount. Emphasise that they should use time phrases, which they should highlight or underline.

Differentiation
For less able children, prepare sentence strips for each event in the cartoon. Help them to arrange the sentences in the correct order and then choose time phrases to add to each. More able children could use the Internet to locate an item of relevance to their history work (for example, film footage of an historical event) and write a recount of this, focusing on using time phrases.

Cloud burst sentences

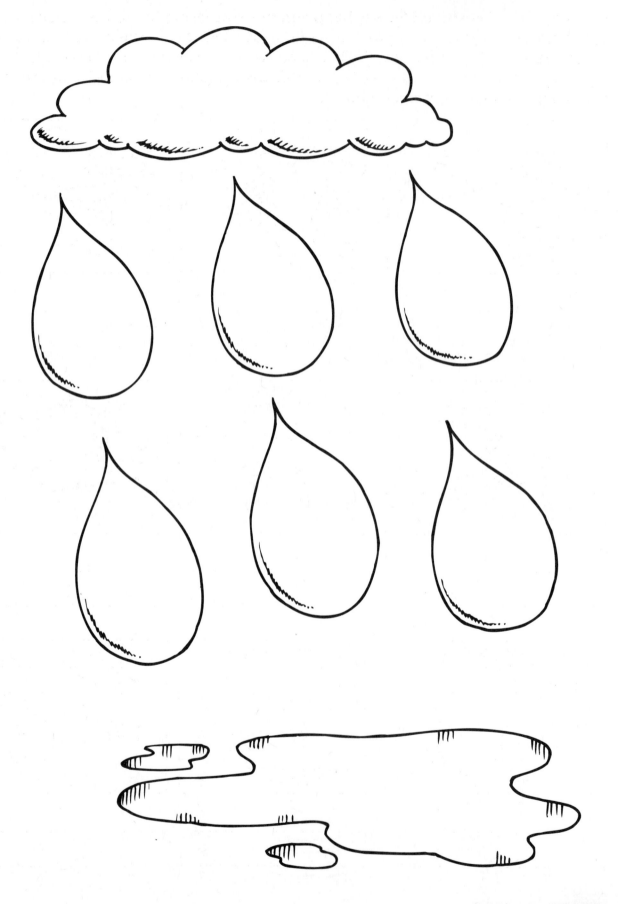

Grammar and
Punctuation
Lifesavers

Spot the stop!

it was a sunny day and molly was happy granny was taking her to the sandcastle competition molly was going to make a fish and cover it with shells she found a space on the beach granny collected shells in a bucket they used pebbles to give the fish a big smile the judges looked at all the models molly and granny won second prize they had a big ice-cream on the way home.

_____ _____ _____

_____ _____ _____

_____ _____ _____

_____ _____ _____

_____ _____ _____

_____ _____ _____

Double trouble

Police shot man with knife

Stolen painting found by tree

Kids make healthy snacks

New vaccine may contain rabies

Local school truants cut in half

Hospitals sued by 7 foot doctors

Include your children when baking cakes

Woman gets 9 months in violin case

Two soviet ships collide, one dies

Deer kill 17 000

Killer sentenced to die for second time in 10 years

Teacher strikes idle kids

Grammar and
Punctuation
Lifesavers

Complex definitions

Verb

A "doing" or "being" word. Verbs give a sentence its action, or they describe the feeling the subject has. They are also about "existing" or "being".

For example, *I am the best!*

Complement

A complement tells you something about the subject.

For example, *The chips were very greasy.*

Subject

The subject is the person, animal or thing about which something is said. The subject usually carries out the action.

For example, *The fireworks lit up the sky.*

Object

The object is the person, animal or thing affected by the action in the sentence.

For example, *The father cuddled the baby.*

Main clause

A main clause has a subject and a verb, and can stand alone as a sentence by itself.

For example, *The clown laughed.*

Grammar and
Punctuation
Lifesavers

Complex definitions

Simple sentence

A simple sentence has only one clause.

For example, *The baby gurgled.*

Compound sentence

A compound sentence has two clauses of equal importance (main clauses). The clauses are joined by and, or, but, yet or so.

For example, *Please be seated and a waiter will take your order.*

Complex sentence

A complex sentence has one main clause, and one or more subordinate clauses. The main clause should be used as the building block on which to build the rest of the sentence – but it can go anywhere in the sentence.

For example, *Do not undo your seatbelt until the green light flashes above your head.*

Clause

A clause expresses an event or a situation. It has a subject and a verb.

For example, *The whistle blew. She was very tall.*

Subordinate clause

A subordinate clause is a clause that cannot be a sentence by itself.

For example, *Do not open the presents until we arrive.*

Grammar and
Punctuation
Lifesavers

Complex creations

● What to do

  (a) Use different colours to identify different parts of these complex sentences:
      Main clause = red
      Subordinate clauses = blue
      Connectives and commas = green

  (b) Separate the complex sentences into simple sentences (HINT: you may have to change one or two words).

  (c) Create a complex sentence of your own using the same sentence structure as each of the complex sentences below.

1.

(a) Daisy, who was the tallest girl in her class, was an excellent netball player.

(b) _____

_____

(c) _____

2.

(a) Although it was night, the white snow and the full moon lit up the countryside.

(b) _____

_____

(c) _____

3.

(a) The hungry troll, who hadn't eaten for days, drooled when he spotted the little Billy goat trotting towards his bridge.

(b) _____

_____

(c) _____

4.

(a) Even though he remembered locking it, Old Tom checked the door once more before he went upstairs to bed.

(b) _____

_____

(c) _____

5.

(a) Holding his rod tightly, David began to reel in the enormous fish.

(b) _____

_____

(c) _____

Order, order!

1. The boy was flying a kite .

2. Amy had lost her school bag .

3. The fireman was holding the hose .

4. The sticky treacle pudding tasted wonderful !

5. It was a dark , starry night .

6. She wore a pretty pink ribbon .

7. Luckily , he had kept the address .

8. The whistle blew , at last !

9. On the bed , there lay a pile of presents .

10. The giant angrily rose to his feet .

CHAPTER 3

Punctuation

AGE RANGE 5–6

LEARNING OBJECTIVE
To use a capital letter for the start of their own name.

CURRICULUM LINKS
NLS: Year R

Capital caterpillar

What you need
A board and writing materials; photocopiable page 71, enlarged to A3 and mounted on card (enough for one per child); small circles of light green card (2–3cm diameter), enough for each letter of each child's name, with dark green card circles for each child's initials; a caterpillar head and tail drawn on card for each child; pens; coloured pencils.

What to do
● Before the lesson, write each child's name on the circles in black felt pen – one letter on each circle. Write their initials in large capitals on the two dark green circles. Muddle the circles up and place them in an envelope with the child's initials on for your reference. Put a caterpillar head and tail into each envelope, too.

● At the start of the lesson, go around the class and ask the children to tell you their first name. Then repeat, asking for their surnames.
● Explain that the first letter in their name is their initial and it always has a capital letter. Go through the alphabet and ask the children to put their hands up if their first name begins with a certain letter. Write their names on the board as the children raise their hands, emphasising the use of the capital.
● Repeat with their surnames, writing them next to their first names.
● Let the children watch you make a completed caterpillar with your own name, mounted on the card and illustrated with legs and tentacles.
● Write your name on the lines in the flowers and butterflies in the border (one letter per space) so that the children can see where they are going to practise writing their own names.
● Give each child their envelope and an A3 copy of photocopiable page 71 on card. Explain that they should sort their caterpillars into the correct order and lay them on the card with the head and tail. Check the names and then stick the caterpillars down, letting the children draw on the legs and tentacles.
● The children can then practise writing their names in the flowers, and colour the picture.

Differentiation
More able children can write their own names on the circles. For less able children, write their names faintly in the flowers for them to go over.

AGE RANGE 5–6

LEARNING OBJECTIVE
To use a capital letter for the personal pronoun 'I'.

CURRICULUM LINKS
NLS: Year 1, Terms 1 and 2
National Curriculum History: Chronological understanding (1a), Knowledge, skills and understanding (6)

This is me!

What you need
A board and writing materials; photocopiable page 72, enlarged to A3, enough for one per child and another copy per child mounted on card; pens; drawing materials.

What to do
● Ask the children to bring into school one photograph from each year of their life. Alternatively, they could draw a photograph-sized picture of themselves (with their parents' or carers' help) taking part in an event that took place in each year of their life.
● Request a note of what was happening in each photo/picture as well as a note of which year it represents in the child's life. This will be useful for your reference and to help jog the children's memories.
● Write a big capital *I* on the board. Explain to the class that when they write about themselves they use a capital *I* because they are important!
● Tell them that for each picture, you want them to write a sentence beginning with *I* to say how old they were, and a sentence saying what was happening in the photo. Write a couple of examples on the board: *I was born in 1999. I was just a tiny baby here; In 2000, I was one. Here I am at the seaside.*
● Give out a paper copy of photocopiable page 72 and indicate where the sentences should be written. Emphasise the use of the pronoun *I*.
● When the children have completed their sentences, and they have been checked, give them the photocopiable page mounted on card and allow them to write their sentences up on it.
● When these have been checked and corrected, stick the pictures into place and then laminate and trim each one. The work makes an excellent table-mat for a child and can be used as a stimulus for talking about happy memories at meal times!

Differentiation
Less able children can have their sentences written in rough for them to copy up on the card version. Allow more able children to write in more detail if they wish. They could also write about what they would like to do when they are older. For example, *When I am 10, I would like to go on a roller coaster.*

AGE RANGE 5–6

LEARNING OBJECTIVE
To use a capital letter for the start of a sentence.

CURRICULUM LINKS
NLS: Year 1, Terms 1 and 2

Alphabet sentences

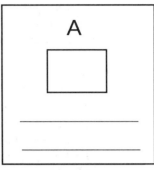

What you need

A board and writing materials; simple dictionaries; whiteboards or paper; pens; 26 pieces of A4 card, each with a large capital letter of the alphabet in the top third, (one for each letter of the alphabet), a blank box in the centre and lines for sentence writing in the bottom third (see diagram); a bag containing the alphabet in plastic capital letters.

What to do

● Go through the alphabet with the children, using your own method – an alphabet song or rhyme. Then discuss upper and lower case letters. Write the alphabet in both cases on the board. For example, *A a, B b, C c.*

● Explain that when we start a sentence we begin with a capital letter. Tell them that the objective of the lesson is to produce twenty-six sentences – each one beginning with a different letter of the alphabet.

● Ask each child to pick a letter from the bag of plastic letters (or two letters depending on how many children there are in the class). They will find this fairer and more fun than simply being told which letter they are going to work on. They can then use the dictionaries to find a word beginning with the letter they have picked. This is a good opportunity to also introduce the term 'noun', if it is appropriate.

● Then ask them to write a sentence in draft on a whiteboard or in a draft book, beginning with their noun. For example, *Apples are good for you, Butterflies are insects with pretty wings.*

● Give each child a prepared sheet which corresponds to the letter they have chosen, and while waiting to have their sentence checked, they can draw a picture relating to their sentence in the box in the centre.

● Check the sentences with the children before instructing them to write up the sentence on the sheet. Emphasise the capital letter at the start of the sentence.

● The twenty-six sheets can then be put up around the class to make an alphabet sentence display.

Differentiation

More able children can take on more letters of the alphabet if necessary. Less able children should work in a group with adult assistance.

AGE RANGE 7–8

LEARNING OBJECTIVE
To use capitalisation for titles, headings, book titles, and so on.

CURRICULUM LINKS
NLS: Year 3, Term 2

A capital collection

What you need
A board and writing materials; photocopiable page 73, enlarged to A3, enough for one per pair; a decorated shoe box; card dividers with headings; smaller, blank cards to fit into the shoe box; a pen on a string; pens.

What to do
● Label a shoe box *Capital Collection* and decorate it with capital letters in different colours and sizes. Place dividers in the box labelled *Titles*, *Book titles*, *Film titles*, *Abbreviations*, and so on. Behind each divider, place a number of cards for the children to write on. Attach a pen to the box with string.
● At the start of the lesson, brainstorm with the children all the occasions when capital letters are used. Try to make the list as extensive as possible and include people's names, titles, initials, the personal pronoun *I*, place names, names of organisations, abbreviations, days of the week, months of the year, planets, book titles, film titles.
● Write each of these in an idea bubble on the board, with branches off for the children's examples, in the same way as the photocopiable sheet.
● Ask the children to make a few suggestions for each category. Help them with categories that may be less familiar to them, such as organisations.
● When you have at least one example for each category, ask the children to continue this on their own using the photocopiable sheet in pairs. Ensure that they do not simply make an extensive list of people's names – set a limit on this category!
● Ask each pair to provide you with some of the examples they have added and add some of these to the board.
● For the plenary, introduce the shoe box. This can be an ongoing feature in the class. The children can add new examples they encounter as well as putting in corrections from their written work. For example, if a child forgets to put a capital letter when needed in their writing, use an agreed format which tells them to correct it and add the example to the Capital Collection box. At intervals throughout the term, the class can have a look to see what has been added to the box.

Differentiation
Less able children could be given a selection of words which need capital letters to add to the correct group on the photocopiable sheet. For more able children, ask them to work on abbreviations for organisations and to add these, with an explanation, to the Capital Collection box.

AGE RANGE 5–6

LEARNING OBJECTIVE
To recognise full stops when reading and understand how they affect the way a passage is read.

CURRICULUM LINKS
NLS: Year 1, Terms 1 and 2

Next stop please!

What you need
A board and writing materials; a Big Book, with one picture and one sentence per page, at a level the children can read themselves; the Big Book story written out in one paragraph, with a large space between each line – photocopy one for each child; coloured pencils.

What to do
● Draw a full stop on the board. Ask if the class knows what it is and why we use full stops. Explain that its function is to mark the end of a sentence, and to tell the reader to pause and take a breath before beginning the next sentence. To make an analogy, explain that sentences are like bus journeys and the full stops are like the bus stops, where people can get on and off.

● Tell the children you are going to read them a story and that you want them to listen very carefully to how you read it, particularly when you stop to take a breath at the end of a sentence.

● Read the story, slowly but with appropriate expression. At the end of the story, ask the class if they think they spotted when you arrived at the full stops.

● Hand out copies of the story and ask the children to read it and highlight the full stops. Write the word *Stop* on the board and tell the children to write this above every full stop.

● They should then practise reading the story by themselves, making sure that they stop for a breath at each full stop.

● When the whole class is ready, ask for their help as you read the story again. Ask them to follow their copy and call out *Stop!* when you arrive at a full stop. Emphasise that this is when you take a breath each time and then continue with the next sentence.

● Individuals can volunteer to read the story to the class. Give positive feedback every time the child stops at a full stop.

● This can be followed up with copies of other texts for the children to search for full stops. They can highlight the full stops with coloured pencils and then read aloud in pairs, using the highlighted full stops to help them.

Differentiation
Ensure that the follow-up texts meet the reading ability of the children.

AGE RANGE 5–7

LEARNING OBJECTIVE
To use full stops to demarcate sentences.

CURRICULUM LINKS
NLS: Year 1, Terms 1 and 2

Full stop flower power

What you need
A board and writing materials; coloured card cut into large petal shapes (enough for four or five per child); black card for the flower centres; green card for leaves and stems; paper; pens.

What to do
● Write a list of the children's favourite colours on the board and then ask them to think of objects in their favourite colour. Write up some of their suggestions. Encourage the children to be descriptive and help expand their suggestions.
● Ask the children to choose their favourite colour. Tell them you want them to write four or five sentences beginning with their colour. For example, *Yellow is the golden summer sun, Yellow is a ripe banana.* Explain that they will write each sentence onto a card petal in that colour – starting at the outside and ending the sentence at the inside of the petal. They will not finish with a full stop, however, as the black circle in the centre of their flower will be the full stop.
● Demonstrate by placing a black circle of card in the centre of the board. Explain to the children that this is what a full stop looks like and that it will also form the centre of your flower. Around the full stop, place four or five petals and write colour sentences in them. Explain to the children how the black circle forms a central full stop for each sentence.
● Give each child some card petals and a black centre, a stem and leaves.
● When they have completed their sentences and created their flower, they should write out each sentence on paper, making a point of placing a full stop at the end of each sentence. The sentences could be displayed beneath each child's flower.

Differentiation
Encourage more able children to be more abstract in their descriptions. For example, when choosing colours such as red, discuss the association with anger. Less able children may produce simple sentences, not necessarily beginning with the colour name.

Yellow is a ripe banana

Yellow is the golden summer sun

Grammar and Punctuation Lifesavers

BRIGHT IDEAS

AGE RANGE 5–7

LEARNING OBJECTIVE
To learn to add question marks to questions.

CURRICULUM LINKS
NLS: Year 1, Term 3

I wonder and I wonder...

What you need
A board and writing materials; *Why Do Stars Come Out at Night?* by Annalena McAfee and Anthony Lewis (Red Fox); paper and drawing materials or a digital camera and computer drawing package; pens.

What to do
● Ask the children if they have ever asked their parents or carers a question that they have not been able to answer! Explain that we ask questions when we want to know something. Draw a question mark on the board and explain that questions are special sentences that have a question mark at the end instead of a full stop. Encourage the children to draw a question mark in the air with their fingers several times.
● Read the book with the children. On one page the book asks the sort of question that a child might ask, and an imaginative answer is given on the next page.
● As you read the book, stop after each question and write it up on the board. Ask the children what needs to be added at the end each time (a question mark). Put in the question mark and ask the children to draw an imaginary question mark in the air with their fingers.
● Encourage the children to come up with answers to the questions before turning the page to see the answer the book gives.
● After sharing the book, brainstorm the sorts of things the children may want to learn more about. For example, dinosaurs, the planets, the tides, volcanoes. Then ask the children to come up with their own *I wonder...?* question.
● Publish the children's questions. Take a digital photo of each child looking puzzled, load the photos into a software program and superimpose a thought bubble above their heads. Print them off so that the children can write their sentence in the speech bubble. Alternatively, cut out a large speech bubble for each child to write in and then arrange these above a cartoon drawing of each child looking thoughtful.

Differentiation
More able children could come up with answers to their *I wonder...?* questions, in a similar manner to the book. Less able children can simply ask questions. To an extent, the depth of question which the children come up with will mean that differentiation is by outcome.

AGE RANGE 6–7

LEARNING OBJECTIVE
To turn statements into questions, learning a range of 'wh-' words typically used to open questions: *what, where, when, who, which, why.*

CURRICULUM LINKS
NLS: Year 2, Term 3

What a picture!

What you need
A board and writing materials; a picture book or poster with 'busy' illustrations (*Where's Wally?* by Martin Handford (Walker Books) would be ideal); paper; pens; a digital camera; a printer; computer software such as PowerPoint or a presentation book.

What to do
● Depending on the resource you choose (books or a poster), show the children a 'busy' picture that shows lots of things going on, such as any page from *Where's Wally?*. Ask them to tell you what they can see.

● Write their statements on the board. For example, *There is a blond-haired boy leaning against the lamp post.*

● When you have a range of statements, explain that these statements could be changed into questions.

● Ask the children if they can give you the six main question words: *what, when, why, where, who and which.*

● Demonstrate how to change one of their statements into a question. For example, *Where is the blond-haired boy? What is the blond-haired boy doing? Who is leaning against the lamp post?*

● Ask for volunteers to change the statements into questions. Write the questions they suggest beside the statements. Highlight the spelling and use of the different question words and keep reminding the children that a question needs a question mark!

● The children can then make up a list of their own questions using the 'busy' picture.

● Use a digital camera to take photographs of the children in different locations around the school, or let the children work in small groups to create their own photographs (with adult supervision). Ensure that every child is included in at least one of the photographs. The photos should be humorous and include lots of detail.

● The children can then create questions for their photographs.

● Load the photographs into a presentation program and create a slideshow with the questions written beside them. Alternatively, print off the photographs and let the children either write or type up their questions, then mount them in a presentation book and create a title page.

Differentiation
Group less able children together when creating their own questions and provide help with the spelling of unfamiliar vocabulary. More able children could be encouraged to write questions that will require the respondent to use inference. For example, *Why do you think Amy is hiding behind the PE store?*

AGE RANGE 6–8

LEARNING OBJECTIVE
To compare a variety of forms of questions.

CURRICULUM LINKS
NLS: Year 2, Term 3

Who's asking?

What you need
A board and writing materials; photocopiable page 74, one per child; pens.

What to do
● Explain to the children that a question is a special sort of sentence that usually requires a response from the person to whom it is directed. There are three main types of question:
  1. Questions for information.
  2. Questions for permission.
  3. Questions that are polite demands.
● Provide the children with examples of each. For example:
  1. *Can you tell me the way to the railway station, please?*
  2. *Please may I leave the dinner table?*
  3. *Will you please keep the noise down?*
● Discuss with the children the sorts of questions that they often ask their parents or carers, and write these on the board. This may provide a good opportunity for combining literacy with PHSE work.
● Then turn the discussion around and ask the children to suggest the sorts of questions they are often asked by their parents and by their teachers, and write some of these on the board. Discuss which categories the different questions fall into – information, permission or polite demands.
● Hand out copies of photocopiable page 74. Ask the children to join the questions to the characters and to write *Information*, *Permission* or *Polite demand* on the line, depending on which type of question it is.
● The children can then work independently to write their own questions for the people listed on the photocopiable sheet.

Differentiation
Work with more able children and introduce the concept of 'open' and 'closed' questions. Ask them to identify which of the questions on the sheet are closed questions (where the answer can only be yes or no). Less able children could just carry out the first part of the exercise.

AGE RANGE 6–9

LEARNING OBJECTIVE
To understand the purpose and use of the exclamation mark to indicate great emotion, such as surprise, joy or shock.

CURRICULUM LINKS
NLS: Year 2, Term; Year 3, Term 1

Wow!

What you need
A board and writing materials; photocopiable page 75, enough for one per child; pens.

What to do
● Ask the children if they know what is meant by an emotion. Explain that our emotions are how we feel about things.
● Ask the children situation questions to provoke different emotions. For example: *How would you feel if you were going out for a picnic and it began to rain?* (Disappointed.) *How would you feel if you broke your favourite toy?* (Angry/hurt/sad.) *How would you feel if you got lost in a busy shopping centre?* (Scared/ frightened/ alarmed.) *How would you feel if you had a surprise birthday party?* (Happy/surprised/ embarrassed.) Write the emotions the children suggest on the board as they arise.

● Explain that sometimes when we feel strongly about something and we feel one of these emotions, we make an exclamation. This is a kind of sentence (an utterance) but is usually quite short and sometimes does not have a verb.
● Explain to the children that when we write an exclamation it ends with an exclamation mark. Demonstrate an exclamation mark on the board.
● Go back to the above questions and ask the children to suggest what exclamations they may say in the situations. For example: *Oh no! Help! This is great!* Write their suggestions up in speech bubbles with exclamation marks.
● Hand out a copy of photocopiable page 75 to each child. Tell the children to look at the pictures and think about what is happening in each. They should decide how the person is feeling and choose the correct emotion from the list. They should then choose an exclamation to put in the speech bubble.
● Discuss the sheet at the end of the activity. If some children finish earlier, ask them to scan through books to find exclamations. They can record these and share them with the class in the plenary.

Differentiation
For more able children, extend the work by asking them to write exclamations that would suit different situations. For example, *What would you say if you fell out of a canoe? What would you say if you saw somebody stealing something?* Provide less able children with a speech bubble with an exclamation in it. Ask them to draw an appropriate picture to go with it and explain the situation to you. They should then have a go at producing a picture and exclamation themselves.

AGE RANGE 6–7

LEARNING OBJECTIVE
To identify speech marks in reading and understand
their purpose.

CURRICULUM LINKS
NLS: Year 2, Term 2

I say...

What you need
Photocopiable page 76 copied onto acetate; OHP; highlighter pens;
copies of differentiated texts with two characters and plenty of speech, one for each
group of three; highlighter pens.

What to do
● Place the acetate copy of photocopiable page 76 on the OHP and cover up the
narrative part, leaving the cartoon for the children to see.
● Ask the children what a cartoon is. Explain that it is a story in pictures where the
words spoken by the characters are shown in speech bubbles and their thoughts in
thought bubbles. Explain that when we see words in a speech bubble coming from a
character we know that that is what the character is saying.
● Ask the children who the two characters in the cartoon are. How do they know? Ask
how we know where the story is taking place (the pictures tell us). Let two volunteers
take on the roles of the two characters and read the cartoon.
● Explain that when we write a story, there are no pictures and so we cannot use
speech bubbles. Explain that we use speech marks around the words that a person says
and dialogue words, such as whispered or shouted, to express how they were said.
● Reveal the narrative and read it to the class. Point out how the words make the
pictures in our minds and the speech marks have replaced the speech bubbles.
● Ask for a volunteer to highlight the words spoken by the two characters – the words
inside the speech marks.
● Ask for volunteers to read the narrative, using one person as the narrator and two
different volunteers as the characters. Repeat this with three different sets of volunteers
until the children understand that the speech marks are used to mark the spoken word.
● Put the children into groups of three and hand out copies of text with plenty of
speech in. Ask them to read the text and work out who the two characters are. Tell
them to use a different colour to highlight the words spoken by each character.
● The groups should then practise reading the text aloud, taking turns to take on the
role of the narrator and the different characters.

Differentiation
Put the children into groups of similar ability and ensure that each group is given an
appropriately differentiated text.

AGE RANGE 7–9

LEARNING OBJECTIVE
To learn the basic conventions of speech punctuation.

CURRICULUM LINKS
NLS: Year 3, Term 1
ICT: QCA Unit 3A, Combining text and graphics

Character quotes

What you need
Internet access; a printer; a board and writing materials; pens.

What to do
● During an ICT session, go onto a suitable website, such as the CBBC website (www.bbc.co.uk/cbbc) or one linked to a current history project. Show the children how to print out a free picture from a website and invite them all to print off one picture each of a favourite character. Alternatively, the children could bring in a picture of someone from a newspaper, magazine or comic.
● Ensure that the children know who their character is and have an idea of their personality. Collect in the pictures.
● To prepare for the activity, cut the pictures out, mount them on A4 paper and draw a large speech bubble coming from the character's mouth. Below the picture, draw three lines for the children to write on.
● At the start of the lesson, explain to the children that when we quote what somebody says, we write or say their exact words. When a quote is written down, the words that have been spoken are put inside speech marks or quotation marks.
● Put a picture of your choice on the board (perhaps of the Prime Minister or a famous historical character), draw a speech bubble and insert a quote.
● Ask the children to tell you the words that the character spoke.
● Write these on the board in one colour. Then use a different colour to demonstrate how to use speech punctuation. Use the following:
    1. Open speech marks.
    2. A capital letter.
    3. A comma, full-stop, question mark or exclamation mark at the end of the piece of speech.
    4. Closed speech marks.
    5. A dialogue word, such as shouted or exclaimed, and the name of the speaker.
● Repeat this with a different quote to ensure the children know the five stages.
● Give the children their characters and let them write their character's quote in the speech bubble and then write the quote as text underneath.

Differentiation
More able children can be taught how to place the dialogue words at the beginning or in the middle of the speech. They should also be encouraged to use adverbs to describe how the words were spoken.

Grammar and
Punctuation
Lifesavers

AGE RANGE 7–9

LEARNING OBJECTIVE
To use speech marks and other dialogue punctuation appropriately in own writing.

CURRICULUM LINKS
NLS: Year 3, Term 3

Quote me

What you need
A board and writing materials; photocopiable page 77, the speech and punctuation cards prepared on A4 card; individual whiteboards; pens.

What to do
● Revise the basic conventions of speech punctuation with the class. Write an example on the board, such as *'Your exam results were excellent. Take the day off!' declared the jolly headteacher.*
● Go through the punctuation with the children:
  1. Open speech marks.
  2. A capital letter.
  3. Speech.
  4. A full stop, comma, exclamation mark, question mark (as appropriate).
  5. Close speech marks.
  6. A dialogue word.
● Select five volunteers to be the Punctuation People. Ask them to stand at the front and give them the punctuation cards (one child will have the full stop, comma, question and exclamation marks, and the others will have one card each).
● Ask for an actor. Choose a confident member of the class who will use expression. Give them a speech card.
● Ask for a volunteer to be a scribe. Pick a more able child to be the scribe to begin with so that the rest of the class understands what is involved.
● When the actor has looked at the speech card, ask them to tell the class who they will be, for example a father. Tell them they should act out what is on the card. For example, whisper softly *Be quiet, you'll wake the baby.*
● Ask the class to write down what the actor said as dialogue on their whiteboards.
● Ask the scribe to write what the actor said on the board. As they do this, ask the Punctuation People

to step forward as the scribe uses each part of the speech punctuation that corresponds to their card.
● Confirm with the class whether the scribe has written the speech up correctly. Get them to hold up their own and check it with the scribe's version.
● Repeat with different volunteers.
● This could be made into a competition by awarding the children points for each correct piece of speech punctuation.

Differentiation
This activity can be differentiated by assigning roles appropriately – less able children can hold up the punctuation cards and more able children could take turns to act as the scribe in front of the class.

AGE RANGE 9–11

LEARNING OBJECTIVE
To learn how dialogue is set out.

CURRICULUM LINKS
NLS: Year 5, Term 1

Dialogue hunt

What you need
A board and writing materials; a selection of books suitable for different reading abilities; paper; pens; highlighter pens.

What to do
● Revise the conventions of dialogue punctuation with the children. Write an example of a piece of dialogue on the board and then present it in different ways. For example:
  1. *'The little boat didn't stand a chance. It was dashed against the rocks,' sighed the lighthouse keeper, shaking his head sadly.*
  2. *Shaking his head sadly, the lighthouse keeper sighed, 'The little boat didn't stand a chance. It was dashed against the rocks.'*
  3. *'The little boat didn't stand a chance,' the lighthouse keeper sighed sadly, shaking his head, 'It was dashed against the rocks.'*
● Ask the children to explain the differences between these three examples (the words are the same but re-ordered, which has an impact on the punctuation). Highlight the punctuation marks and draw up rules as a class. Also draw attention to the use of adverbs and interesting alternatives to the word said.
● Explain to the children that if a second speaker replies, then their speech starts on a new line.
● Put the children into pairs and ask them to either choose books from the library, use their own reading books or work from books that you have pre-selected. Explain that their task is to scan through the books and find a piece of dialogue for each of the three styles on the board. Their choice of dialogue should also be dictated by interesting choice of dialogue words and use of adverbs.
● Tell the children they should copy out their chosen pieces exactly and then highlight the punctuation. They should be prepared to explain each piece of punctuation and explain the use of new lines.
● Ask the pairs to share their findings and select favourite examples to write up on the board. Run through the rules of dialogue presentation using their examples.
● For homework, or in a follow-up lesson, ask the children to write a piece of dialogue between two characters, in each of the three styles above, starting on a new line for each new speaker.

Differentiation
For less able children, write out the dialogue without any punctuation and set them the task of punctuating it. Select challenging texts for more able children to scan through.

Grammar and
Punctuation
Lifesavers

BRIGHT IDEAS

AGE RANGE 6-8

LEARNING OBJECTIVE
To use commas to separate items in a list.

CURRICULUM LINKS
NLS: Year 2, Terms 2 and 3

When I went on holiday...

What you need
A selection of objects associated with seaside holidays, such as a bucket and spade, sunglasses, a rubber ring; a board and writing materials; paper; pens; dictionaries, enough for one per group of five to six children.

What to do
● Ensure that the children can all draw a comma. Explain that a comma is a punctuation mark that is used to separate parts of a sentence and that it can be used to separate items in a list.

● Ask if the children have ever played the game 'When I went on holiday… '. Explain the rules. The first player begins, saying *When I went on holiday, I packed in my suitcase a…* and they suggest an item. The second player then repeats this and adds an item. This continues until one of the players forgets one of the items on the list or makes a mistake. They are then out. The game continues until only one player is left.

● Tell the children they are going to play the game. Lay out all the holiday items at the front of the class as a stimulus. Write the starting sentence up on the board. For example, *When Class 3 went on holiday, they packed in their suitcase…*

● Select volunteers to play the game until you have six or seven items. Stop the game and explain that you are going to write up the items into a list, using commas to separate them. Complete the sentence on the board demonstrating the use of the commas clearly. Explain how to end the sentence using *and* before the last item and point out that this doesn't have a comma before it. For example, *When Class 3 went on holiday, they packed in their suitcase a beach towel, sun-cream, a speedboat, a rubber ring, a bucket and a pair of shorts.*

● Put the children into groups of five or six and let them play the game. Each group should then write up their list, using dictionaries for unfamiliar vocabulary and ensuring that they punctuate their sentence correctly.

● As a plenary, allow each group to show their list and as a class check whether each group has punctuated their list correctly.

Differentiation
For more able children, insist that they use one or more adjectives to describe their items. Less able children can use items with vocabulary labels on to help remind them of the list and to assist them when writing.

AGE RANGE 8–9

LEARNING OBJECTIVE
To understand how the comma is used to mark grammatical boundaries in a sentence.

CURRICULUM LINKS
NLS: Year 4, Term 1; Year 5, Term 1

Famous inserts

What you need
A board and writing materials; photocopiable page 78, enough for one per child; pens.

What to do
● Draw a comma on the board and ask the class what it is and what they think it is used for. Explain that it indicates where the reader should take a short pause in order to ensure that their reading makes sense. Explain that the comma is also used to break up longer sentences into smaller chunks and to separate out extra bits of information.
● The last use is the focus of this activity. Write an example on the board, but do not insert the commas. For example, *The postman who drives a red van took the letters to the sorting office.*
● Ask the children which piece of information could be removed to leave a shorter sentence that still makes sense (who drives a red van). Explain where in the sentence the commas should be placed.
● Encourage the children to create some other examples based on the syntax of the above sentence. For example, *The teacher, who was in a very good mood, decided not to set any homework.*
● Once the children have grasped the concept of separating out extra information within a sentence using commas, hand out photocopiable page 78. The ten short sentences, each one about a famous person, has an extra piece of information which the children can insert into the sentence between two commas.

Differentiation
More able children can go on to write their own sentences about other famous people, using reference books to help them find out factual information. Provide less able children with information in order to help them match up the extra information to the correct person.

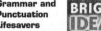

AGE RANGE 7–11

LEARNING OBJECTIVE
To understand when to use the colon to introduce a list, a quotation or a second clause that illustrates the first.

CURRICULUM LINKS
NLS: Year 4, Term 3; Year 5, Term; Year 6, Term 1

Colon completion

What you need
A board and writing materials; library access; photocopiable page 79, enough for one per child; pens.

What to do
● Draw a colon on the board and explain to the children that it has three main uses:
1. To introduce a list.
2. To introduce direct speech, for example a quote.
3. To introduce a second clause in a sentence that illustrates the first one.
● Provide examples of each type of use. For example:
1. *To make a kite you will need: paper, scissors, string and wood.*
2. *The crowd chanted: 'God save the Queen.'*
3. *The man was shaking: he had had a real fright.*
● Give the children a set amount of time to go to the library and scan books for colons. They could work in pairs. Ask them to bring back any examples they find.
● Discuss the examples they found as a class and categorise them as above, writing examples on the board.
● The children can then use photocopiable page 79 to practise using colons. The sheet requires them to complete sentences from the colon onwards, and then to write out their own sentences.

Differentiation
For less able children you may like to adapt the photocopiable sheet so that the sentences are complete but the children have to insert the colon. More able children should be encouraged to create their own sentences, either in addition to those on the photocopiable sheet or instead of them.

AGE RANGE 10–11

LEARNING OBJECTIVE
To secure knowledge and understanding of how to use a semi-colon to separate items in a list that consists of longer phrases.

CURRICULUM LINKS
NLS: Year 6, Term 1

A tasty treat

What you need
A board and writing materials; paper; pens; paper plates, coloured napkins and plastic knives and forks; black ink.

What to do
● Ask the children what they might have for breakfast. Write a list sentence on the board, only writing individual items, and omit the commas. For example, *For breakfast I like to have orange juice toast cereal and yoghurt.* Ask the children to punctuate the sentence, separating items with commas (except before the *and* as the last item is listed).
● Now introduce the semi-colon. Explain that one of its uses is also to separate items in a list, but only where the items consist of longer phrases.
● Return to the breakfast sentence and ask the children to help you to describe the foods in more detail. For example, *For breakfast I like to have freshly squeezed, chilled orange juice; thick slices of toast with butter, strawberry and blackberry jam; cereal covered in sweet, brown sugar and a healthy natural yoghurt!* Explain that because each item is now an adjectival phrase, it needs to be separated with a semi-colon. Ensure the class can see how a semi-colon is written.
● Write another sentence. For example, *At a birthday party you might eat sausage rolls, fairy cakes and crisps.* Expand the detail of the items mentioned. Use semi-colons to separate the new list together.
● The children can then write a list sentence for one or more of the following:
  1. *My favourite lunchtime meal is…*
  2. *For dinner I like to have…*
  3. *If I went on a picnic I would take…*
  4. *At Christmas we eat…*
● They could start by making a simple list using commas. The items in the list could then be expanded into adjectival phrases, separated by semi-colons. Work together as a class to begin with, brainstorming ideas for descriptive phrases, such as *hot crusty bread, crisp fresh lettuce, jam doughnuts oozing with fresh cream.*
● The children could choose their favourite list and write this up using black ink on a coloured paper plate. These could be used as a display with napkins, plastic knives and forks and pictures of food.

Differentiation
Less able children could work in a group with adult assistance to help them expand the items into adjectival phrases. Provide more able children with new, challenging vocabulary to incorporate into their lists. Ask them to use dictionaries to locate the meanings of the words.

Grammar and
Punctuation
Lifesavers

Capital caterpillar

This is me!

	_____
	_____
	_____
	_____
	_____
	_____

Grammar and
Punctuation
Lifesavers

BRIGHT IDEAS

A capital collection

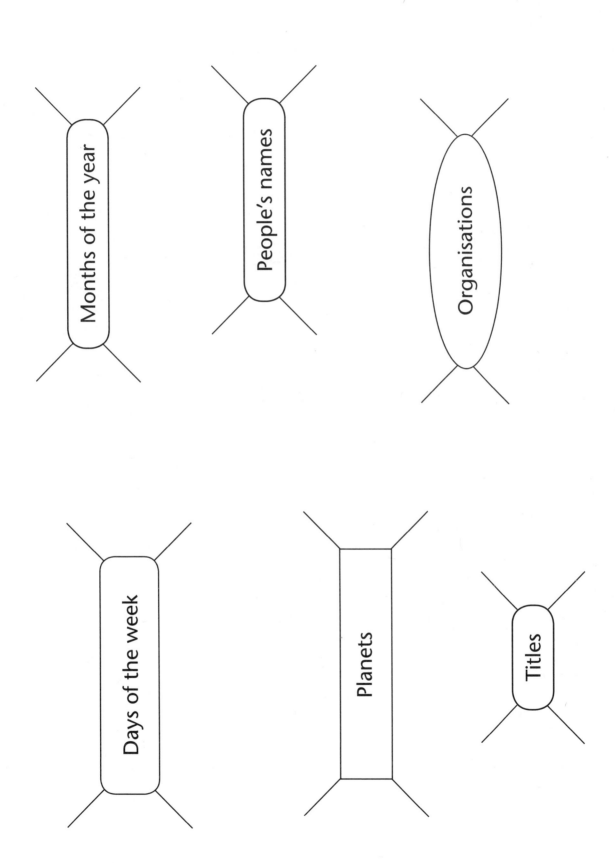

Months of the year

People's names

Organisations

Days of the week

Planets

Titles

Who's asking?

● Join the questions to the person asking them. Write *Information*, *Permission* or *Polite demand* on each line.

Have you brushed your teeth?   Have you done your homework yet?

Please may I have an ice-cream?

Will you tidy your room please?   Will you stop teasing your brother, please?

Teachers	**Parents/carers**	**Children**

Can you read ten pages of your reading book for tomorrow?

How many days are there until Christmas?   When will we be at Granny's house?

Will you please keep the noise down?   Will you sit down?

● Now write a question that you might ask each of the following people:

Teacher

_____

A parent or carer

_____

Policeman

_____

Zoo keeper

_____

Librarian

_____

The Prime Minister

_____

Grammar and
Punctuation
Lifesavers

Wow!

● How is the person in each picture feeling?

1. _____

2. _____

3. _____

4. _____

5. _____

6. _____

7. _____

8. _____

Hurt	Proud
	Disappointed
Happy	Excited
	Scared
Alarmed	Shocked

● Choose an exclamation for each picture from the list below and write it in the correct speech bubble:

Help!	Ouch, that hurt!	Stop, thief!	Oh no!	Look out!
How lovely!		Brilliant, thanks!		I don't believe it!

I say...

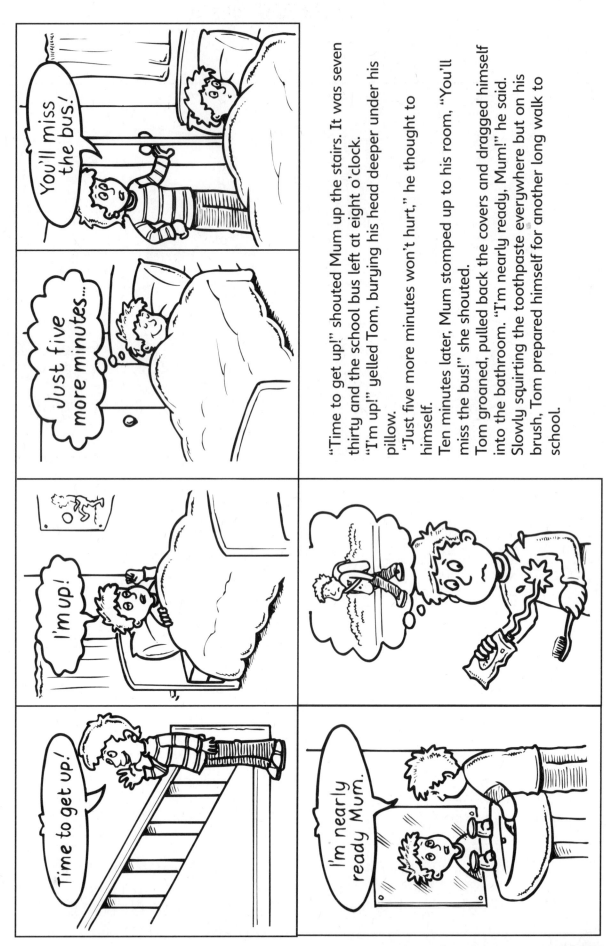

"Time to get up!" shouted Mum up the stairs. It was seven thirty and the school bus left at eight o'clock.

"I'm up!" yelled Tom, burying his head deeper under his pillow.

"Just five more minutes won't hurt," he thought to himself.

Ten minutes later, Mum stomped up to his room, "You'll miss the bus!" she shouted.

Tom groaned, pulled back the covers and dragged himself into the bathroom. "I'm nearly ready, Mum!" he said. Slowly squirting the toothpaste everywhere but on his brush, Tom prepared himself for another long walk to school.

Grammar and Punctuation Lifesavers

BRIGHT IDEAS

Quote me

Open speech marks "	CAPITAL LETTER	!	?
Close speech marks "	Dialogue word and speaker's name	,	.

Speech cards

Copy the speech cards onto individual cards. A blank one has been added for you to copy and create your own examples.

Card 1	You are:	a father
	You say:	"Be quiet, you'll wake the baby."
	This is how you say it:	whisper softly
Card 2	You are:	a naughty child
	You say:	"I don't want to go to bed."
	This is how you say it:	moan and stamp your foot
Card 3	You are:	a policeman
	You say:	"Put your hands up, you are under arrest."
	This is how you say it:	order firmly
Card 4	You are:	yourself
	You say:	"I've won, I've won, I've won!"
	This is how you say it:	shout, and jump up and down excitedly
Card 5	You are:	_____
	You say:	_____
	This is how you say it	_____

Famous Inserts

● Select the correct piece of extra information from the box below and insert it into the sentence using commas.
The first one has been done for you.

1. Florence Nightingale *, who nursed soldiers during the Crimean War,* was known as the Lady of the Lamp.

2. Mother Teresa _____ received the Nobel Peace Prize in 1979.

3. Martin Luther King _____ was assassinated in 1968.

4. William Shakespeare _____ was born in Stratford upon Avon.

5. Ludwig van Beethoven _____ was born in Germany in 1770.

6. Thomas Edison _____ devised the electric light bulb.

7. Winston Churchill _____ became Prime Minister during World War II.

8. Queen Elizabeth I _____ reigned from 1558 until 1603.

9. The Romans _____ invaded England in 55BC.

10. Queen Elizabeth II _____ was crowned in 1952.

---

who nursed soldiers during the Crimean War

composer of thirty-two piano sonatas

the youngest daughter of Henry VIII

an American inventor

who fought for equal rights in America

led by Julius Caesar

who worked in the Calcutta slums

the older daughter of George VI

famous for his cigar and "V for Victory" sign

one of England's most famous writers

Grammar and
Punctuation
Lifesavers

BRIGHT IDEAS

Colon completion

● Insert a colon and then complete the sentences.

1. My favourite television programmes include _____

_____

2. The ingredients for a pancake are _____

_____

4. I have been to the following holiday destinations _____

_____

5. Here is the team for the school quiz _____

_____

6. The sign said _____

_____

7. The message in the card read _____

_____

9. He was so hot _____

_____

10. The girl was happy _____

● Now write three examples of colon use of your own (one introducing a list, one introducing a quote, one introducing a second clause).

1. _____

2. _____

3. _____

CHAPTER 4

Grammatical awareness and presentation

AGE RANGE 7–8

LEARNING OBJECTIVE
To use awareness of grammar to decipher new or unfamiliar words.

CURRICULUM LINKS
NLS: Year 3, Terms 1, 2 and 3

Word detectives

What you need
A board and writing materials; dictionaries; an text extract that has words which are likely to be unfamiliar to the whole class, copied onto acetate; OHP; photocopiable page 90; pens.

What to do
● Ask the children what they can do if they are reading and come across an unfamiliar word. There may be several responses, including ignore it and carry on reading(!), ask an adult or use a dictionary. Point out that often it is possible to guess the meaning of a word by using clues in the rest of the sentence.
● Write a word on the board that you are confident none of the children will be familiar with. For example, *detrimental*. Ask the children to guess what it means. Without putting the word into the context of a sentence, they will have few clues to help them.

● Follow this by writing the word into a sentence. For example, *Too many chips and other greasy foods can be detrimental to your health.*
● Ask the children to guess the meaning of the word and tell you what helped them to make their guess. Let them confirm the definition using a dictionary.
● Show the class the extract on the OHP. Read it together and underline the words that you think will be unfamiliar to the children. As a class, use grammatical awareness to decipher the meaning of the words. Ask the children to use dictionaries to check the meanings.
● The children can then work on their own using photocopiable page 90.

Differentiation
More able children could be given a piece of text containing challenging vocabulary. Let them identify the unfamiliar words, use grammatical awareness to try to decipher the meanings and then confirm these using dictionaries. When working on the photocopiable sheet, read the first ten sentences with less able children to guide them towards working out the meanings. For the second part, provide definitions of the words in the box.

AGE RANGE 9–10

LEARNING OBJECTIVE
To secure the basic conventions of standard English, with respect to the avoidance of double negatives.

CURRICULUM LINKS
NLS: Year 5, Terms 1, 2 and 3

Be positive!

What you need
A board and writing materials; photocopiable page 91; pens.

What to do
● Ask the children if they have ever heard the expression *Don't be so negative!* Ask what they think is meant by this and ask them to think of negative words. For example, *no, can't, don't, won't, nothing, nobody, didn't, isn't.*

● Explain that it is grammatically incorrect in standard English to use two such words in one sentence. Essentially, the negative of a negative is a positive. Therefore, if a double negative is used, the speaker is inadvertently expressing the opposite of what they mean.

● Provide an example on the board, such as *He doesn't want nothing to eat.* Explain that this actually means he does want something to eat – that not nothing, is something! Tell the children that the sentence should read *He doesn't want anything to eat* and write this on the board.

● Hand out copies of photocopiable page 91 to the children and read through the instructions at the top of the sheet with them to ensure they know how to complete it.

● Discuss the answers as a class.

Differentiation
Less able children can identify the two negatives in the sentences on the photocopiable sheet and then explain tasks 2 and 3 verbally before attempting to correct the sentence. Explain to more able children that a negative form can be used with a word with a negative prefix. For example, *The children weren't unkind to the new boy.* Point out how the positive version of this sentence would read *The children were kind to the new boy.* Let them create sentences in the negative form with words with negative prefixes and compare them with the positive alternative. They should discuss the subtle differences in meaning between the two.

AGE RANGE 9–10

LEARNING OBJECTIVE
To secure the basic conventions of standard English, with respect to the agreement between nouns and verbs.

CURRICULUM LINKS
NLS: Year 5, Terms 1, 2 and 3

That book were good!

What you need
A board and writing materials; photocopiable page 92; pens.

What to do
● Write *That book were good!* on the board. Explain that the sentence is not written in standard English, because the verb is in the plural form but the subject is singular (one book). Explain that they are going to learn the rules for ensuring that there is agreement between the subject and the verb in sentences.
● Explain the rules for subject–verb agreement: a singular subject requires a singular verb and a plural subject requires a plural verb. For example, *I am, he/she/it is, you are, we are,* and *they are.*
● Explain that sometimes there are tricky examples where it is difficult to tell whether the subject is singular or plural. For example:
  1. *One of our baby rabbits has been sold.* (The subject is one so it takes the singular verb.)
  2. *A flock of geese flew over the rooftops.* (The subject is the collective noun, which is singular.)
  3. *Tommy and his dog are best friends.* (Two singular nouns are joined by and, making them a compound subject, so they require a plural verb.)
● Explain that mistakes can be avoided when making subjects and verbs agree by checking whether the nouns are 'countable' (singular or plural, so they may take either a singular or plural verb) or 'uncountable' (singular only, so they will only take a singular verb). For example, water and patience are both uncountable nouns and so they take the singular form of the verb.
● Explain that if a singular noun is used in a sentence which is later referred to using a pronoun, the pronoun must agree with the noun. For example, *Skydivers must have nerves of steel; they put their lives in danger every time they jump from the plane.* (The pronoun is plural (they) because the plural noun was used.)
● Provide examples on the board regarding subject–verb agreement and ask the children to help you create a rule for each of the examples. Number the rules so that they can be referred to when using the photocopiable sheet.
● Give out copies of photocopiable page 92 and ask the children to convert the sentences into standard English, ensuring that there is agreement between the subjects and the verbs.

Differentiation
More able children should explain which rule each sentence is breaking when completing the photocopiable sheet. Less able children can highlight the incorrect word.

AGE RANGE 6–8

LEARNING OBJECTIVE
To use standard forms of verbs in speaking
and writing, and to ensure grammatical
agreement between pronouns and verbs.

CURRICULUM LINKS
NLS: Year 2, Terms 2 and 3; Year 3, Term 3

Do you agree?

What you need
A board and writing materials; photocopiable page 4d; pens.

What to do
● Ask a simple question, such as *Where were you last night at 7 o'clock?* Collect the children's answers on the board. For example, *I was in bed, I was in the bath.*
● Play devil's advocate and ask if they were sure they didn't mean *I were in bed* or *I were in the bath?* Ask them to explain what is wrong with your examples. They will probably reply with 'It doesn't sound right'!
● Explain that the examples you gave were non-standard English, as the subject and the verb didn't agree. Explain that in a sentence the subject and the verb must agree.
● Write a simple example on the board, such as *I kicked the ball.* Explain that the subject is the person or thing that goes with the verb. Confirm that *I* is the subject and *kicked* is the verb.
● The children need to know that a singular subject take a singular verb and a subject which refers to more than one person or thing takes a plural verb. This information can be summarised as follows:

These subjects all take a singular verb (am, is, was)
1. I (first person singular)
2. He, she, it (third person singular)
3. Pronouns, such as each, anyone, either, neither, anybody, every
4. Collective nouns, such as a flock of geese

These subjects all take a plural verb (are, were)
1. We (first person plural)
2. You (second person plural)
3. They (third person plural)
4. Combined subjects of two or more people, such as Dad and I

● As a class, practice putting together singular subjects with singular verbs and plural subjects with plural verbs, before providing the children with the photocopiable sheet to work on independently. For example, Is 'he' singular or plural? Yes, 'he' is singular, so 'he' takes a singular verb. For example, *He is eight.*

Differentiation
Less able children can highlight the incorrect word in sentences 1–8 on the photocopiable sheet, and be given a choice of was, are or were with which to replace it. More able children could take a piece of text and attempt to convert it into non-standard English!

AGE RANGE 10–11

LEARNING OBJECTIVE
To understand the features of formal official language and collect typical words and expressions.

CURRICULUM LINKS
NLS: Year 6, Term 2

It's official!

What you need
Examples of both formal and informal communications copied onto acetate, for example formal invitations, a legal document, a letter of complaint; OHP; a board and writing materials; paper; pens.

What to do
● Prior to the lesson, choose two children and help them to prepare two short scenarios where one asks the other to pass the salt during a meal. In the first, they should use language appropriate to eating a meal at home and in the second they should act out asking for the salt at a formal banquet. For example, *Pass the salt would you please, Dad?* and *I am so sorry to trouble you, but would you mind passing the salt please?*

● Open the lesson with the two scenarios. Ask the class to compare the language used and to guess where each scenario was taking place. Explain that we use formal and informal language in different situations according to our audience.

● Provide a list of contexts in speech and writing and ask the children to rate them according to formality. For example, an invitation to a wedding, a letter of complaint about cracked pavements to the Council, a postcard to their granny, a letter in support of a job application, a party invitation from a friend.

● Show the children the examples of communications on the OHP and read through them together. Annotate the text and collect useful phrases. These could be written on the board or in a class notebook for reference on other occasions.

● As a class, compile a fictitious letter from a railway company to a passenger who has written to complain about the service provided. Ask the children whether they think the language should be formal or informal. Useful phrases to add could include, *On behalf of the company...* or *We trust that this will assure you of our good intentions.*

● Let the children write the original letter written by the passenger.

Differentiation
More able children can attempt this task without support. For less able children, supply a letter template with phrases omitted. For the rest of the class, provide a list of phrases which they may like to include in their letter.

AGE RANGE 10–11

LEARNING OBJECTIVE
To identify and know how to use the active and
passive voice.

CURRICULUM LINKS
NLS: Year 6, Term 1

Where's the emphasis?

What you need
A variety of objects to use as props, such as beanbags and balls; a board and writing
materials; a television; a video recorder; two five-minute programmes with lots of action.

What to do
● Before the lesson, choose a group of six or seven children and set up an action
sequence for them to act out. There could be ball throwing, chasing, and so on. Allow
the children to rehearse.
● At the start of the lesson, write a simple sentence on the board and ask the children
to identify the subject, verb and object. For example, *The dog chased the cat*. (*The dog* is
the subject, *chased* is the verb and *the cat* is the object.)
● Explain to the children that this sentence is written in the active
voice. The subject carries out the action. Explain that this is
a more common form of writing, and that it is personal
and informal.
● Explain that when writing or speaking in the
passive voice, the subject is the recipient of the
action – it has the action done to it. Write an
example on the board: *The cat was chased by
the dog*.

● Explain that although the two sentences
have the same meaning, the emphasis is
different. The passive voice is used mainly
when writing scientific and formal reports, and
in multiple choice tests.
● Let the class watch the action sequence that
the group of children have practised and then, as
a class, write up what happened in the active voice.
For example, *Jan chased Hanif, Rob threw the ball to
Megan*. This will be straightforward, as the active voice
is the common way of relating action.
● The class can then practise writing in the passive voice by
making up a multiple choice test for the action sequence. For example:
  1. *Hanif was chased by (a) Ben (b) Rob (c) Jan*.
  2. *The ball was thrown to Megan by (a) the Loch Ness Monster (b) Rob (c) Katy*.
● To follow this up, split the class into two groups. Let each group watch a different
programme. Tell them to take notes whilst watching to record what happens.
● When they have watched the programmes, the groups should make up a multiple
choice questionnaire of what they have seen, writing in the passive voice.
● When you have checked these, the groups can then watch the other group's
programme and answer the associated questionnaires.

Differentiation
Split the groups according to ability, and provide support for the less able group.

AGE RANGE 10–11

LEARNING OBJECTIVE
To conduct detailed language investigations of proverbs
through interviews, research and reading.

CURRICULUM LINKS
NLS: Year 6, Term 3

As the
saying goes

What you need
A board and writing materials; photocopiable page 94; pens; Internet access.

What to do
● Write a well-known proverb up on the board before the lesson, for example, *Two
heads are better than one.*

● At the start of the lesson, ask the children to think about what the proverb means
and to suggest a situation when somebody might use it. For example, when a teacher
has set a difficult problem and the children have asked if they can work together. Make
sure the children understand that the proverb means that when discussing a problem
it is better to work in pairs, because they can share ideas and possibly come up with a
solution more quickly.

● Explain to the children that proverbs are short sayings that are in general use, and
are often used to offer advice. Tell them that proverbs have originated over many
centuries and come from nations across the globe.

● Ask the children to share with the class any proverbs they have heard of. Discuss the
meaning of the proverbs they suggest.

● Give the children a copy of photocopiable page 94. They can work on sections A
and B first and then discuss the work together as a class. The children can follow this up
by completing section C, carrying out their own research using reference books and the
Internet, and also carrying out interviews with relatives or carers.

● *Poor Richard's Almanac* (1732–57) written by Benjamin Franklin (writing as Richard
Saunders) is a good starting point for researching proverbs. The book is full of scraps of
advice, sayings and morsels of wit, many of which were turned into proverbs. These can
be found on the Internet. There are many Internet sites dedicated to proverbs and you
will need to provide suitable web addresses to ensure that the children's searches are
focused and useful. Two sites that are particularly useful are: http://humanities.byu.edu/
elc/student/idioms/idiomsmain.html and http://wiktionary.org/wiki/English_proverbs.

● To develop this activity, the children can choose their favourite proverb and use it
as a title for a short story, or illustrate its meaning with a poster. The stories and posters
they create can be used to create a class book about proverbs.

Differentiation
Less able children should create posters as their follow-up work. More able children
should create stories using proverbs as the subject and moral of their stories.

Too many cooks spoil the broth.

Grammar and
Punctuation
Lifesavers

**BRIGHT
IDEAS**

AGE RANGE 6–7

LEARNING OBJECTIVE
To use a variety of simple organisational devices to indicate sequences, such as arrows, lines, boxes and keys.

CURRICULUM LINKS
NLS: Year 2, Term 1

Let's get organised! (1)

What you need
A selection of books, such as children's craft books or recipe books, where different presentational devices have been used, such as arrows, boxes or keys; cotton wool; cress seeds; marker pens and/or stickers; paints; paintbrushes; water; a board and writing materials; A3 paper; photocopiable page 95.

What to do
● Before the lesson, ask the children to bring in an eggshell in an egg box.
● At the beginning of the lesson, explain to the children that they are going to make cress-head people – a simple activity with clear-cut stages that is fun! Explain that the object of the lesson is to take careful note of how they make their cress-head people. Tell them they will be making an activity sheet afterwards to instruct other children how to make cress-head people.
● Show the children how to make the cress-head people: create a face on half of the eggshell with a marker pen or stickers, fill it with cotton wool, soak the cotton wool with water, sprinkle on the cress seeds, make an egg cup by cutting up the egg box, paint the egg cup, place the cress heads in the dark until the cress seeds germinate, then put them in the light and watch them grow. Tell the children they must keep the cotton wool damp.
● Once this has been done, the children will all have the same practical experience to draw on for their literacy work.
● Show the children the range of books and discuss the different presentation devices that have been used.
● Discuss what will be needed on an instruction sheet for making cress-head people. This could include a list of materials, numbered stages detailing what to do, diagrams linked by arrows, and symbols as a reminder to water the cress heads.
● List all the materials that the children used to make the cress-head people on the board, and write sentences for each of the stages. Encourage the children to tell you what you should write.
● Provide the children with a sheet of A3 paper and let them write their own instruction sheet.

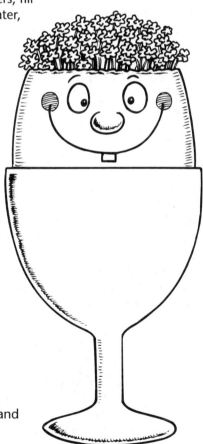

Differentiation
More able children can work on blank sheets and create their own instructions. Less able children could be given photocopiable page 95 to fill in.

Let's get organised! (2)

AGE RANGE 6–8

LEARNING OBJECTIVE
To use a range of other ways to present texts and explore purposes of headings, sub-headings, captions, enlarged and italicised print.

CURRICULUM LINKS
NLS: Year 2, Term 2; Year 3, Term 1

What you need
Books that illustrate the use of headings, sub-headings, italicised text, and so on; a board and writing materials; A4 paper; rulers; coloured pencils and pens.

What to do

● Once you have carried out 'Let's get organised (1)', the children will have experienced presenting instructions using devices such as boxes, arrows and keys. Based on the same activity, the children can now create a second instruction sheet using a different style of presentation.

● Show the children the books and discuss the use of bold, enlarged and italicised print. Talk about why these are useful and what they tell the reader.

● Work together as a class to create an instruction sheet for the cress-head people. Take suggestions from the children and act as scribe, writing up the instructions on the board. Emphasise the need to use a ruler for underlining and demonstrate how to create headings using capital letters of uniform size. You may like to use the following:

1. Large bold print for the heading.
2. Sub-headings entitled: *What you need, What to do, Diagram.*
3. Bold print for numbering the different stages.
4. Captions for diagrams in italics.

● When the class have created this second instruction sheet, they can compare this style of presentation with that in 'Let's get organised (1)' and discuss the relative merits of each style.

● The children can copy what they have created as a class and use this as a model for future independent work.

● The children could also search through reference books and find examples of different presentation forms that they feel are particularly effective. They could bring what they have found to a class discussion, and decide which presentation devices they think they will use in their own work in the future.

Differentiation
More able children can work independently. Less able children can use ICT with an adult before attempting to write up the work themselves.

AGE RANGE 10–11

LEARNING OBJECTIVE
To conduct detailed language investigations
through interviews, research and reading.

CURRICULUM LINKS
NLS: Year 6, Term 3

English through the ages

What you need
Photocopiable page 96; extracts from Beowulf, Chaucer's Canterbury Tales and Shakespeare (enough for one per child); Internet access; access to the library; an etymological dictionary.

What to do
● The English language has been influenced by many different events during the history of the British Isles. The children will be aware of a number of these historical periods as a result of their history studies throughout Key Stage 2.
● Give the children a copy of photocopiable page 96, and use it as a reference point for a discussion about the history of the English language and its origins.
● To demonstrate to the children how the English language has changed throughout history, give them the text extracts. Encourage the children to try to spot words that they recognise and discuss how these have changed.
● The children can then use the photocopiable sheet as a stimulus for carrying out a search for words that entered the English language during each of the historical periods. They can record the words they find in the last column on the photocopiable sheet.
● To help the children, you may like to provide them with words and ask them to find out where they came from. The following would be interesting:
    1. Words originating from Scandinavian sources: *dream, skirt, water, strong, reindeer, husband, calf, outlaw.*
    2. Words of Norman influence: *beef, jury, verdict.*
    3. Words introduced by Shakespeare: *leapfrog, dwindle, majestic, critical.*
    4. Words introduced from Hindi sources during the rise of the British Empire: *bungalow, dungarees, pyjamas, jodhpurs, shampoo, jungle, loot, polo.*
    5. Words originating during the Industrial Revolution from Latin and Greek roots: *oxygen, protein, nuclear, vaccine.*
    6. Words adopted from maritime influences: *blockbuster, camouflage, roadblock.*
● To make a display of this work, annotate a world map with coloured arrows showing the countries of origin of the words. Add details of the events in history that led to their adoption into the English language.

Differentiation
Provide less able children with reference material that you know contains information about words and the English language. Also provide Internet site addresses for them to search through. Allow more able children to carry out a more extensive search without assistance.

Word detectives

● Read each sentence and then choose a word from the box to replace the word that is underlined.

1. After playing football all morning, the young boy was so hungry that he <u>consumed</u> everything on his plate.
2. The firework display was a <u>spectacular</u> sight to behold!
3. The <u>impertinent</u> pupil had to stay in at break time as a punishment for his behaviour.
4. With the <u>surplus</u> material, Mum made some cushions to go with the curtains.
5. The girl was <u>absent</u> from school because she had chicken pox.
6. Some people think bungee jumping from the top of a tall building is a <u>ridiculous</u> thing to do!
7. "Who broke my window?" shouted the <u>irate</u> shopkeeper.
8. Meena was <u>petrified</u> because she had to go into hospital for an operation.
9. Jim was <u>ecstatic</u> when he heard that he had passed all of his exams.
10. The ride whizzed round and round and the children became very <u>giddy</u>.

silly	away	happy	extra
angry	see	scared	
dizzy	rude	wonderful	ate

● Now try these:

1. The pilot flew the little plane back to the _____.

2. A city has a bigger _____ than a village.

3. We were given _____ to go out to play.

4. When we are ill, the doctor gives us a _____ for some medicine.

5. The wheels on a lorry _____.

rotate	prescription
permission	
population	aerodrome

Grammar and Punctuation Lifesavers   BRIGHT IDEAS

Be positive!

● Underline the two negatives in the sentences below.

● Write what the sentence literally means.

● Write the grammatically correct form in standard English.

1. She said she didn't want nothing for it.

Literal meaning: _____

Grammatically correct sentence: _____

2. Nobody here knows nothing about a robbery.

Literal meaning: _____

Grammatically correct sentence: _____

3. I didn't do nothing wrong – it was him!

Literal meaning: _____

Grammatically correct sentence: _____

4. I can't do nothing about it.

Literal meaning: _____

Grammatically correct sentence: _____

5. It hasn't got nothing to do with me.

Literal meaning: _____

Grammatically correct sentence: _____

6. Nobody knew nothing about the new housing project until the lorries started arriving.

Literal meaning: _____

Grammatically correct sentence: _____

That book were good!

● Convert these sentences into standard English:

1. The cat were chasing the mice all around the garden.

_____

2. The exam were harder than I thought it would be.

_____

3. The dinner were spoilt because we was late.

_____

4. One of the teachers are going to take the class on a field trip.

_____

5. One of the apples were rotten.

_____

6. A herd of cattle were crossing the road so we had to wait until they had passed.

_____

7. Mum and I was doing the cleaning when the doorbell rang.

_____

8. Rosie, Sam and Yan was in the same team on sports day.

_____

9. I burnt my toe because the bath water were too hot!

_____

10. The violence in the crowd at the football match were out of control.

_____

11. A tiger is a valuable commodity to some societies: they are being hunted to extinction.

_____

12. Dad's patience were running out, he didn't like being kept waiting.

_____

Grammar and
Punctuation
Lifesavers   **BRIGHT IDEAS**

Do you agree?

● Convert the following examples of non-standard English into standard English.

1. I were happy when my team won the cup.

_____

2. Mother and baby is both doing well and will come out of hospital soon.

_____

3. He were good at maths, but I were better.

_____

4. They was naughty and the teacher kept them in at playtime.

_____

5. My friend and I was having an argument when the bell rang.

_____

6. The cat were very agile, it jumped over a very high wall.

_____

7. It were a brilliant party!

_____

8. Anyone were allowed to have a go.

_____

● These sentences are written in standard English using singular subjects. Make the subject plural and change the verb to ensure that they agree. The first one has been done for you.

1. The girl is happy   ⟹ *The girls are happy.*

2. The dog is barking.   ⟹ _____

3. The mouse likes cheese. ⟹ _____

4. The boy is kicking a ball. ⟹ _____

5. He was shouting very loudly. ⟹ _____

6. She is top of the class. ⟹ _____

7. The bird was singing sweetly. ⟹ _____

8. I am seven years old.   ⟹ _____

Grammar and Punctuation Lifesavers

As the saying goes

Section A.

Match each proverb below to the sentence in the box that has the same meaning.

1. You can lead a horse to water, but you can't make it drink.

2. Don't judge a book by its cover.

3. A problem shared is a problem halved.

4. When in Rome, do as the Romans do.

5. Beauty is in the eye of the beholder.

6. Look before you leap.

7. Two wrongs don't make a right.

8. Every cloud has a silver lining.

9. Better safe than sorry.

10. More haste, less speed.

A. You shouldn't make a decision about something because of what it looks like on the surface.

B. When you are visiting somewhere, you should respect and adapt to local customs.

C. People see beauty in different ways – one person may see something differently to another.

D. Think carefully about what you are doing before you begin.

E. If somebody hurts you, it won't make it better by hurting them.

F. When something bad happens there is usually something good to come out of it.

G. If you hurry too much you will make mistakes and end up taking longer, as you will have to put the mistakes right.

H. You can provide a person with opportunities, but if they choose to ignore you there is nothing you can do about it.

I. Don't take unnecessary risks.

J. It's good to talk to someone when you have a problem as it can help to make it better.

Section B.

Write your own definitions for the following proverbs:

1. A chain is only as strong as its weakest link.
2. It's no use crying over spilt milk.
3. Don't put all your eggs in one basket.
4. Laughter is the best medicine.
5. You can't teach an old dog new tricks.
6. It's no use locking the stable door after the horse has bolted.
7. Don't bite the hand that feeds you.

Section C.

Use the Internet and reference books to collect other proverbs. Ask your parents, carers or grandparents for any proverbs they know. Ensure that you find out what the proverbs mean and when they might be used.

Grammar and
Punctuation
Lifesavers

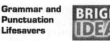

Let's get organised!

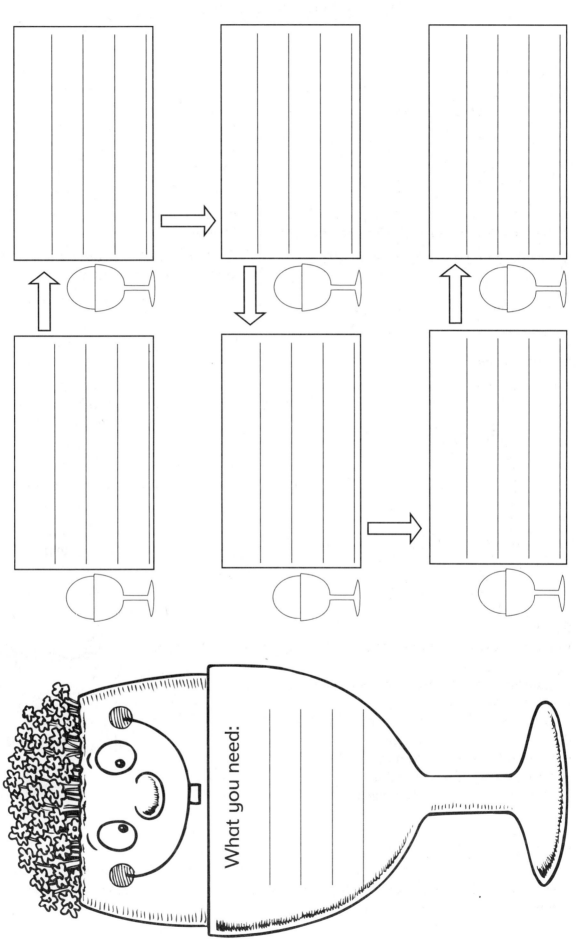

What you need:

English through the ages

Language and examples to look at	Period	Historical events	Influence	Words originating during this period
Old English. Poem: *Beowulf*.	500–1100 AD	Invasion and settlement by the Angles, Saxons and Jutes from Jutland and Southern Denmark. Invasion by the Vikings.	Old English – the Celtic speaking inhabitants were pushed out of what is now England, into Scotland, Wales, Ireland and Cornwall. North Germanic words.	
Middle English. Chaucer's *Canterbury Tales*.	1100–1500 AD	The invasion and conquest of England by William the Conqueror – Duke of Normandy.	The invaders spoke a language known as Anglo-Norman which is a dialect of Old French. The influence of Latin was also great.	
Early modern English. Shakespeare.	1500–1800 AD	The Renaissance – the revival of classic scholarship. The advent of the printing press. William Caxton brought it to England in 1476. The life and works of Shakespeare.	Latin and Greek words. The printing press meant that books were cheaper and English became standardised, in terms of fixed spelling and grammar. The first English dictionary was published in 1604. Shakespeare introduced over 2000 words and many catchphrases into the English language.	
Late modern English.	1800–present day.	The rise of the British Empire. The Industrial Revolution. The two World Wars in the 20th century.	Britain adopted many foreign words. The British Empire was based on the maritime and so there was a strong influence of nautical terms. The rise in technology meant that there were many creations and discoveries that needed new names. These mainly originated from Greek and Latin. Military influence was great.	

Grammar and Punctuation Lifesavers